GOD is a DJ*

* but he only warms up for
SASHA!

GOD is a DJ*

* but he only warms up for
SASHA!

by
Brendan Blood

with Foreword by
Vernon Kay

Dawber Publishing
2011

© Brendan Blood 2011

Published in the UK by Dawber Publishing 2011

All rights reserved. No part of this publication may be reproduced, stored in a retrieval system or transmitted by any means, electronic, mechanical, photocopying or otherwise without the prior consent of the authors.

A catalogue record for this book is available from the British Library.

ISBN 978-0-9563353-6-4

Printed in the UK by
CPI Antony Rowe, Chippenham, Wiltshire

CONTENTS

List of Plates	vii
Foreword	ix
Introduction: Box of Delights	1
The Interview	6
1 Delight: Shelley's Laserdome, Longton, Stoke, 1990/91	11
2 Solstice: Manchester Academy, July 1991	31
3 Haçienda Night: Ministry of Sound, London, 1992	39
4 Harmony: Haçienda, Manchester, 1992	45
5 Up Yer Ronson/SOAK: Corn Exchange, Leeds, 1992/93	57
6 Venus/Renaissance: Nottingham/Mansfield, June 1993	69
7 Cream and the Big Apple: 1995–2002	78
8 Bedrock First Birthday: Heaven, London, October 1999	96
9 We Love Sundays: Space, Ibiza, September 2000–2002	102
10 Midweek Session: Club Code, Birmingham, October 2000	115
11 Tribal Sessions: Sankeys Soap, Manchester, 2001–2003	125
12 Circus: Masque, Liverpool, June 2005	143
Epilogue: The Warehouse Project, Manchester, 2006–2010	158
Track Listing	178
Discography	182
Thanks	185
Contributors/Photos/Recommended Reading/ Recommended sites	186

Plates

Between pages 54 and 55

1 Hidden gem: Those in the know knew where to go – Hackett's, Blackpool, 1990.
2 Living the dream: Delight at Shelley's Laserdome, Longton, 1990.
3 Not to be missed: The year 1991 was an incredible one for Venus, a club that never failed to deliver the best in house music.
4 Hot date: That one Saturday a month was always worth the two-hour drive – the drive back was rubbish though!
5 Bringing glamour to house: The Corn Exchange was an incredible venue to match the crowd it attracted.
6 Grand finale: The last night of the Northern Exposure Tour, Leeds, 1995.
7 Amazing venue: Shopping in Leeds would never be the same again – The Corn Exchange, 1991.
8 He's back: Sasha's first residency since the closure of Shelley's in 1991 – the original Renaissance at Venue 44, Mansfield.
9 Forget the weekend: This was what the middle of the week was all about – The Haçienda, 1992.
10 What Fridays were all about: Shine at The Haçienda, 1992.
11 Urban icon: The Haçienda, Manchester, 1986–1997 – RIP!
12 Landmark disc: The original mix CD that became the benchmark for what others could only dream of achieving.
13 Shape of things to come: But Sasha hated this *Mixmag* cover from February 1994.
14 A true 'Summer of Love': It's 1991 and *Mixmag* brings Sasha to the masses whether he likes it or not.
15 A step forward: The night Sasha launched the groundbreaking Pioneer CDJ2000.
16 Road trip: The Delta Heavy tour of America with John Digweed, 2002.
17 Sign of the times: A landmark set that confirmed Sasha had gone digital – Circus at The Masque, Liverpool, June 2005.
18 At one with the crowd: Sasha in action, April 2008.
19 Honorary guest: A landmark night in the history of the Ministry of Sound, September 2009.
20 The cream of Manchester: The Warehouse Project logo.

God is a DJ*

Between pages 150 and 151

21 Cooling down: Sasha takes a minute, Jacksonville, Florida, USA, 1999.
22 The box of magic: Sasha at work in Jacksonville, 1999.
23 The main event: Sasha enthrals another main room, this time at Space, Ibiza, 1999.
24 Turning heads: Live at Café Mambo, Ibiza, Summer 2002.
25 Taking a minute: Tanned and relaxed while launching the awesome *Global Underground* mix at Café Mambo.
26 Night games: The twilight hours at Twilo, New York, 2005.
27 Rising to the top: Sasha at Cream, Liverpool, 2002.
28 Vital equipment: If these headphones could only talk, what a story they would tell – Sankeys, Manchester, 2003.
29 When vinyl ruled the world: Another legendary set at Tribal Sessions, Sankeys, Manchester, 2003.
30 Eastern promise: Sasha playing to the masses live in Bucharest, 2005.
31 The magician reveals his tricks: Sasha's technical rider, 2005.
32 Sun kissed: Sasha is that good, he can even get the sun to set with the flick of a switch – Miami Boat Party, March 2006.
33 Happy Days: When Sasha smiles, so does Shanghai. A sign he has gone truly global, 2005.
34 I love my job: Sasha battles on at Le Souk in New York despite distractions, 2006.
35 Milking the crowd: . . . and they bloody love it. Sasha & Digweed, April 2008.
36 Remember this? Sasha at Amnesia, Ibiza, August 2007.
37 Brewing up a storm: Sasha at The Warehouse Project, December 2007.
38 Prime pairing: Sasha and John Digweed took America to the next level with their landmark Spring tour, 2007.
39 A dream come true: The beautiful Paula Pedroza with her idol talking all things house, 2010.
40 In the zone: Live in the mix at the Haçienda 25th anniversary at Urbis, Manchester, July 2007.
41 Me and him: The author with Sasha at Urbis, Manchester, during a July 2007 celebration night marking 25 years since the legendary Haçienda opened.

FOREWORD

WHEN I was asked to write the foreword to this book, I tried to think of some nice things to say about Brendan. Then I realised that all I had to say were nice things.

I first came across Bren around 1989 in a club called Legends, which was underneath Warrington rugby league ground. It was a tiny sweatbox of a club with a low ceiling, smoke machine and '80s glitz décor, and was one of my, and many others', first hunting grounds in our search for dance music clubs.

However, we all knew Brendan was a veteran of the warehouse raves in Blackburn, and if he was there, it was a good recommendation.

Most other northern clubs were by now playing our favoured big piano anthems which we could blow our whistles to, but Legends became exactly what it said and evolved into the focal point of our mundane working week. Within a short space of time, everyone knew each other, and many of us remain friends today.

As with all good things, it came to an end and this little known raver's paradise closed, but the sadness didn't last too long as we all moved onwards and upwards to the Mecca known as the Haçienda. I was a Saturday night regular worshipping the legendary Graeme Park whereas Bren preferred his more serious Friday nights with Mike Pickering. We still kept in touch throughout at our regular Sunday night hang out, The Tavern on the Hill, where we caught up on 'the best nights of our lives'.

Our circle of friends grew through various clubbing excursions up and down the country. Most of us lived within a five-mile radius of each other, hence the strong northern accents amongst us. It proved hard not to bump into each other at someone's 21st birthday party or the local pub. But if you wanted to know what was hot or who was not then you only needed to ask Bren. He always knew where the next new big venue was going to be and what that massive record you'd heard at the weekend was called. If there was something going on, he knew and he'd be there at the opening of an envelope! Having sampled virtually every club in the North West, there was no one better qualified than Bren to put on a party of his own.

God is a DJ*

His first effort, the 'Ace of Clubs' all-nighter held at his local football club, will go down in history. It was an invite-only event by word of mouth, but with the amount of people Bren knew, it was always going to be a lock-out.

Along with my mates, Sean, Luke, Simon and Mez, we turned out in '70s fancy dress with the biggest of collars and the tightest of tank tops. The others wore wigs whereas I just blended in! Everyone we knew was there, with our mates DJing and playing all our favourite Haçienda classics and more.

The 'committee men' who were serving behind the bar continued to do so until it ran dry. This happened at around 5am and I am proud to say I bought the last drink in the house. How we got home I've no idea, but everyone still talks about those parties to this day. Bren has continued putting his organisational skills to full use with Ace of Clubs now entering its 16th year, and I'm proud to say I was there at the very start.

Since those early days I've gone on to do some television and radio work that some of you may have seen or heard. I even found time to marry my girlfriend, Tess Daly, and make inroads into starting a family with the addition of our beautiful daughters, Phoebe and Amber. But I still love to get on that dance floor when the mood takes me. Whatever I get invited to, be it a party, an award ceremony or the premiere of a movie, I am always safe in the knowledge that I can invite Bren along. No matter who we meet along the way, be it the driver picking us up, the runner for the TV crew or Cameron Diaz, he'll always be polite, sociable and great company to be with, treating each person with equal respect.

This book provides all who were there, or those wishing they had been, with a great insight into what has made dance music the phenomenon it still is today.

I'd guess a lot can't remember last year, let alone the last decade, so thank God that Brendan can!

Vernon Kay

INTRODUCTION

Box of Delights

FROM the age of four when I came home with my first ever piece of vinyl, Mud's *Tiger Feet* from Woolworth's, and played it on my dad's record player, I was hooked on music.

After probably a whole weekend of playing the same record over and over again till I was word perfect, I wanted to play something else that I had not heard before. From then on, I was always searching for something new and inspiring to listen to, be it pop, soul, reggae, punk, rock or just plain weird. It wasn't that important what genre of music it belonged to as long as it had a beat and a melody.

This went on for a few years under the supervision of my mum and dad, who put the records on for me, until I was eventually bestowed with my very own record player. I then had most of Motown and Rod Stewart's best tracks at my disposal. I blame my mum for the latter but it was an education nonetheless.

The first album I ever bought was disco 'pirates' Boney M's *Nightflight to Venus* in 1979, when I was eight years old. Maybe I was just killing time between then and 1987, when house music broke through in the UK, but listening to such a diverse selection of music during my formative school years stood me in good stead for a movement that was to be a life-changing experience.

With an assortment of Abba LPs and my own fascination with glam rock, soft metal and anything electronic, I had sampled most forms of popular music.

During my school years, my best friend Gareth would try to get me to listen to The Smiths and The Cure but whilst not wanting to shout about it, I had a flirtation with soft rock legends Bon Jovi, Heart and Bryan Adams. Conversely, we both found middle ground with the likes of Queen, Bob Marley, Depeche Mode and New Order.

Throughout our teens they would all subconsciously mould our musical tastes for what the future held. This nurturing time proved invaluable when I encompassed the fresh, exciting sounds that emanated from Chicago, Detroit and New York, together with everything Italy could throw at me, as I came to realise that house

God is a DJ*

music had been born. I consider myself one of the lucky ones to have embraced this movement at such an early stage.

The inception of house music, which derived from the discos of New York in the late Seventies, was extremely well documented and researched in the Channel 4 series 'Pump up the Volume'. The whole scene at that time amalgamated black with white, straight with gay and the corrupt with the clean. This was the first time such a diverse mix of people had gathered under one roof to share in the delights of a new phenomenon.

Although heavily fuelled by drugs such as MDMA in its purest form, acid and amyl nitrate, it was the music, championed by New York legend Larry Levan along with Ron Hardy and Frankie Knuckles that took people on a journey they never knew existed. The journey usually lasted from early Saturday evening through to the early hours of Monday morning for those lucky enough to know where the party was. People from all walks of life and backgrounds shared life-changing experiences with people they would never have crossed paths with before.

The end of disco had morphed into the beginnings of 'house' as the major players involved in this movement sampled and experimented with different ways of making music to move you. Intrigued by those sounds emitting from New York, Chicago and Detroit, it didn't take long before influential British players such as New Order together with then unknown UK DJs Pete Tong and Paul Oakenfold made frequent journeys over to the 'Big Apple' to sample the delights of this new found faction.

They not only returned with a box full of records but a whole new attitude and outlook that would change the way we perceived our stale and stagnant discotheques with their Eighties glitz and chintz accompanying the wisecracking smooth lines of what we then knew as a 'disc-jockey'.

Gareth and I endeavoured to listen to, record and buy as much house music as we could embrace to feed our new found addiction. Like two sponges, we soaked up every morsel of club culture to the point where we knew what we wanted, where to go, how to find it, where to get hold of it and most importantly, who we preferred to listen to. And the name that constantly appeared at the top of both our lists was Sasha.

Introduction

From hearing him play at illegal raves in disused warehouses around Blackburn and Colne and other venues in the industrial wastelands of Lancashire, the name stuck with me. I didn't know whether his name was spelt 'Sasha' or 'Sacha', but I knew he played my kind of music. However, once the police had intervened on the warehouse scene in the summer of 1989 by introducing the Criminal Justice Bill, it put the frighteners on all would-be promoters and organisers alike. The Bill stated that any unlicensed party that played 'sounds, wholly or predominantly characterised by the emission of a succession of repetitive beats' would have all equipment confiscated indefinitely and fines and arrests would be made.

During this period of unrest, we tried to make as many 'Sasha' gigs as we could. Even a five hour car journey wouldn't deter us, such was our faith in his music, although others, quite content with their local 'Ritzy' nightclub, would gag in disbelief at the lengths we would go to JUST to hear someone play records.

The need to let more people know about this house music phenomenon that was sweeping Britain brought about the idea of our own fanzine in the guise of 'Ace of Clubs', which proved to be our catalyst into the sound we took as our own. It was filled with humorous articles – well, in my opinion anyway – and an in-depth knowledge of who was playing where and who wasn't. But what we really required was an interview with a major name player on the circuit. This would enable us to make an impact on what was quickly becoming a saturated market of fanzines from Brighton to Aberdeen. When I said big name, five letters was perfect. To get an interview with Sasha for the first edition would be a dream come true.

Wheels were set in motion when we obtained the telephone number of his then manager James Baillie, a promoter who ran Venus in Nottingham, which at the time was one of the most successful underground house nights in the UK. We had made our visits to Venus a regular monthly pilgrimage, such was our thirst for new, enticing nights which were now cropping up at an alarming rate. And this one was always worth the wait.

James, with ginger, cropped hair and small in height but not in presence, with a personality to match his demeanour and dress code, was as accommodating as his night and had passed on our interest in pursuing an interview directly to Sasha.

God is a DJ*

Whilst enjoying the delights of Gareth's mum's cooking one Friday night before our weekly pilgrimage to Shelley's, the phone rang. His mum answered politely then called Gareth to the phone.

"It's for you," she said. "Someone called Sasha is asking for you."

The look on our young, innocent faces must have been a real sight to behold. I still get excited thinking about that moment in his mum's kitchen, even as I'm writing this. The conversation was pretty brief as I remember, but the more I have got to know Sasha over the following years, I realised most conversations with him are, mainly due to the ever increasing demands on his time accompanied by his somewhat reserved demeanour. A time and date was set to go round to his place of residence at the time, which was in Fire Station Square, Salford.

Mixmag had recently done an article on the man they proclaimed 'Son of God' and the 'first pin up DJ', labels he had hated from the time they were published. This was not the kind of publicity that sat easily on such young, unassuming shoulders.

To lighten his mood we had a life-size cardboard cut-out made of the so-called pin up DJ, with the torso of a Chippendale transposed onto his then ponytailed head. The journey to his abode with cardboard dummy stood upright in the back of my Astra convertible that Monday night turned a few heads in Salford to say the least, but not nearly as much as the amount my stomach was turning as we came within reach of the aforementioned Square.

The Chippendale Sasha, incidentally, came to a premature end at a party back at Sasha's after one of his gigs at the Haçienda. It was stood behind his decks in the living room and one of Sasha's mates, Buckley, became a little paranoid with the dummy, insisting its eyes were following him round the room, and so decided to literally knock its head off.

Back to that nervous night, and tentative knocks on No. 24 followed after a routine of 'you knock, no you knock', before the legend that is Sasha opened the door in his industry standard black T-shirt, stonewashed jeans and black industrial boots, hair in ponytail of course.

On entering the house, we made hesitant introductions as I quickly scanned the deep, rectangular, double-sized living room to find a distinctive split. The front section comprised two well-worn sofas in each corner, which I was sure had been well received by the clientele that had frequented these sagging cushions on many a night's come

Introduction

down. But the rear of the room was the bit that captivated my imagination as I fixed my stare on the right hand wall, decorated in vinyl from floor to ceiling. The discs were all very neatly arranged but unfortunately we later found out they were in no particular order whatsoever, much to our and I presume Sasha's dismay.

As we got comfy on the hallowed sofas, the interview commenced with some light hearted banter, both parties as diffident as each other, but gradually he seemed to warm to our straight man/funny man routine à la Morecambe and Wise.

The only omission from the following reproduction of the interview as it appeared was my never to be forgotten embarrassing question "So what's your real name?" which still grates with me to this day. Thankfully I wasn't the first and I won't be the last to ask it.

This interview, almost 20 years ago, was the beginning of a long-standing friendship, which has now encapsulated years of clubbing experiences involving Sasha, all of which have been more than a pleasure to be part of. Hopefully some of you reading this will have been part of some of the special nights I am about to impart to you, rekindling some fond memories that you didn't realise you had.

For those of you too young to be there, this is just a sample of what you've missed so far . . .

THE INTERVIEW

Originally published in 'Ace of Clubs' fanzine, 1991

BACK in early 1988, a certain young man would make the weekly trip from his home town of Bangor to the legendary Haçienda to hear the musical talents of then residents Jon DaSilva, Graeme Park and Mike Pickering.

Nothing unusual in that I suppose, but eventually he himself would be setting the very same dance floor alight with his own DJing skills. A man called Sasha, not Adam.

I grew up and discovered house music in the Haç. I made it just in time for the smiley T-shirt/acid house explosion.

So how did he first get started from clubber to DJ?

Well, I eventually moved up to Manchester in March 1988. Bangor was horrible really. I had a normal job but sacked that after a short while and made daily visits to 'Eastern Bloc' (the most upfront, influential record shop in Manchester at the time), hounding them for the latest tunes.

I moved into the same block of flats as Jon DaSilva and he used to get loads of offers but had to turn some gigs down due to his workload as there weren't many house DJs around at the time, so he would pass them on to me.

A stroke of luck methinks, but I'm a great believer in making your own luck in this world.

With the record collection increasing daily, so were the one-off nights which eventually led to his first regular club night, every Friday at Bugsy's in Ashton.

"The club was totally wild!" he enthuses. Running at the same time as the (in)famous Thunderdome, the club, with a capacity of 400 split on two floors, would be packed to the rafters with the same regulars who previously frequented the Dome on a Saturday.

The next regular night to become accustomed to Sasha's own brand of DJing, with heart-rending vocals and chonking piano intros, was the legendary Shaboo in Blackpool. This ran concurrently with the warehouse days centred round Blackburn.

The place was absolutely mental from start to finish! It could go on till 3 or 3.30am armed only with a licence till 2am. It was mad, I used to do a five hour set all on my own.

So did you manage to get up to the warehouse parties?

Only in the last few weeks as I was usually knackered from the DJing. I managed to get on the decks when it started to get really big so I suppose that's why some people think I was one of the main Blackburn DJs.

Two months after the closure of Shaboo, Sasha took his box of delights to Shelley's Laserdome in Stoke.

I loved that club. The crowd was perfect who both knew and appreciated my tunes. I could play a mellow set, like Corina etc, have them in the palm of my hand, then build it up.

But with the massive success of the night, both the crowds and the media attention grew.

i-D magazine did a feature, amongst others, and soon the place started to get full of idiots. Kids with no tops on coming up to you saying 'Give us some Techno!' Even some of the warm up DJs started to get carried away playing massive tunes at 11 o'clock. That was the time to get out.

His work has taken him to various places round the world including Ibiza, America, Japan, Australia and this summer Rimini.

The Japanese clubs are amazing! One called 'Gold' has seven floors, with a different theme in each like sumo wrestling and a love room. The lift from the entrance brings you up to the dance floor, it's just wicked!

Back in Britain he's just getting busier by the week with regular spots at his beloved Haç as well as Venus, Kinky Disco and Soak to name but a few.

His new baby is now Renaissance at Venue 44 in Mansfield. **The Restoration of Sasha to the North of England** states the flyer in bold. Mansfield in the North? You may argue but there's no questioning its

God is a DJ*

huge success with an endless line up of top quality DJs and PAs from around the globe.

> It was just the venue I was looking for, an all-nighter on a Saturday throughout the summer.

Since Sasha started DJing he has become immensely popular both at large raves as well as the small intimate clubs, but how and why?

> It's weird I know. I've stopped doing the big ones for now. They seem to have become too hardcore, although I will do the big one offs like Pushca in London. The people seem more intelligent about the music, like you could play a Talk Talk track and people would appreciate and probably know the record whereas at a big rave they would just stop and say 'Give us some more hardcore!!'

Having such a massive following in the North, what has been the reaction to you down South?

> It's getting there slowly. I think people became a little prejudice against me because of the *Mixmag* interview, even though I haven't played there much. But now with me doing Pushca, Kinky Disco, Shave Yer Tongue and the Ministry of Sound once, hopefully it will change people's perceptions.

What's your view of the club scene down there?

> London seems to be very divided, whether you're into a particular DJ or a certain club. You don't float about, whereas in the North people seem to be more prepared to travel about.

In the December issue of *Mixmag*, a certain headline has given Sasha, it seems, no end of grief. 'The First Pin-Up DJ' read the front cover. He groans when I reiterate the headline.

> The last few issues had Seal, Lisa Stansfield and the Pet Shop Boys, so when I was asked: 'Do you want to be on the cover of *Mixmag*?' I thought 'Wow! You want me to be on the front' If I had turned it down, I would only have regretted it. But I hated the title and the pictures that went with it. The interview was more about hero-worshipping. It prejudiced me against people

The Interview

> *I've never met because once they've met me, they know I'm not like that at all.*

Sitting with him in his front room, watching early Comic Strip videos, I assured myself how right he was as you couldn't meet a more down to earth person. Even though he didn't necessarily approve of the interview and how he had been portrayed, the offers of work from Australia, Singapore, Switzerland, Berlin and more came flooding in.

With such a busy schedule in Britain and abroad, do you still find time to search for records?

> *I've got a good relationship with John from Eastern Bloc who'll put records aside and get a box to me each week depending on where I am at the time. I also get sent loads of records (up to 70 in a good week). 60 per cent are usually crap but I very rarely throw any away.*

Looking at his record collection crammed into the shelves along the back wall of his house, I can well believe it. It will probably put your average record store to shame.

> *I don't get chance to send in chart returns due to my schedule and so used to get kicked off their mailing list every couple of months, but it seems I'm lucky now because of who I am. When I come across the people sending them out I try get round to thanking them just to show I appreciate it.*

And what about time to practise?

> *I need a couple of days a week out of the studio to practise my mixing otherwise it does my head in. Only then can I feel ready and confident for the coming weekend gigs.*

Practice makes perfect as they say, and he rarely gets it wrong on the night, which is why the name Sasha guarantees a full house whenever his name appears on a flyer, which seems like every other one printed at the moment! So what does he make of his 'cult' following?

> *Wicked, I love it. It gives me a great buzz, people you've never met before coming up to you, shaking your hand. Ultimately, I think it's a sign of respect.*

God is a DJ*

Unafraid to experiment with different styles of house music, a few surprises are usually on the cards. Steve Bicknell, Terry Farley as well as his early influences Park, Pickering and DaSilva appear to impress Sasha with their fearless approach to DJing and ability to work records beyond their obvious elements as opposed to just playing each record in a straightforward manner. This approach creates a more progressive house scene unlike the hardcore scene that he imagines will become bigger and bigger until it explodes to replace the likes of Kylie and Jason as mainstream pop music.

With the continuing success of Sasha's DJing exploits, his name has also started to appear on record sleeves as a remixer with alarming frequency, which he clearly sees as the way to his future. The first track to incorporate his talents was Evolution's *Came Outta Nowhere*. Matched with his ability to play the piano, which he first learned at school and fortunately continued throughout his adolescence, his remix work now numbers an impressive 30. Two current projects he is working on are for Joan Armatrading and Annie Lennox, such is the esteem he is now held in.

> *The piano has been a great asset in my remix work so far and I'd love to work with someone like The Orb, DOP or Leftfield.*

Somehow I can't see that being a problem.

Future plans include the release of his own album and the progression from DJ to remixer to artist is an idea that really excites him. Working with the likes of PP Arnold, Evolution and his trusted studio engineer Tom Frederickse, he plans to write an eight track mini album. He enthuses about how each track would be perfect in every way from the intro to the last fading beats, but then that's how he operates and what I believe elevates him above the crowd. It's a long way from the usual schoolboy fantasy of wanting to be a footballer, but luckily for clubland that dream faded long ago! Long live the future and whatever it holds?

1

Delight

Shelley's Laserdome, Longton, 1990/91

BY the time I had left secondary education in 1987, MARRS, S'Express and Steve 'Silk' Hurley had become household names, providing a sound that brought my musical tastes to the fore, and by the following year each artist had attained chart success with a Number One to boot.

This format, which was relatively new to the UK, sampled beats and blended melodies to give us a sound we distinguished as house music, or 'Disco's Revenge' as it was so eloquently described by legendary Chicago DJ Frankie Knuckles. And so began our fascination with dance music and all who sailed in it.

Fortunately I looked old enough to get into nightclubs, of which my home town of Leigh had the venue Segars to offer. It was a two level club playing soul, hip hop and rare groove upstairs whilst downstairs was my first real taste of house music courtesy of DJ Stu Allan, who I would like to thank from the bottom of my heart for giving me a great foundation, and also for putting up with me asking for Asmo's *Jam the Dance* and TNT's *Piano Please* every week.

From this humble beginning, both Gareth and I were then on the lookout for something more to satisfy our needs, and lo and behold, so were many other kids of our age in the area. With a constant need for more, people decided to take it upon themselves to make their own parties. However, with no premises or licence there was a necessity to take this forceful youth movement underground, and out of this came the legendary Blackburn raves.

Word spread quickly amongst like-minded people who wanted to party for longer. Disused warehouses around the industrial landscapes of Lancashire became the targets for eager promoters anxious to take the house sound to a bigger stage. Once a suitable sound system had been acquired it was purely down to word of mouth as to where and when it would take place and the crowd would simply follow. The only other requirement was a DJ with a box full of the records we were striving to hear.

These were exciting times for all involved. We were driving in convoys of 500 cars, maybe more, and often dangerously as at times the convoy was on both sides of a dual carriageway. A sea of red lights snaking into the distance could be seen for miles, unless you unfortunately ended up at the front of the pack not having a clue which way to go. The convoy continued well into the early hours of Sunday mornings, searching for that secret location before finally ditching your car and heading for some large, empty and deserted building in the middle of an industrial estate. The thud of a bass bin could be heard in the distance and the glimmer of a strobe would flash in the black of the night each time the warehouse door opened.

The illegal raves weren't interested in having all these fancy lights, it was more about having a smoke machine and a strobe light. That seemed to be enough for a party back in those days,

Sasha's DJ partner John Digweed said of the house movement that swept right across Britain.

It was great just because it was different. There was this energy and not only that, there was a whole unity. All these people certainly got together. We were meeting up week in, week out at different venues just having a great time. At that time it was very much a case of finding a location wherever you could get away with it without the police getting a chance to shut it down. There was always that excitement; I think that's what made it so much fun. You didn't know how long it was going to last, you just had as good of a time as you could.

This situation only lasted for about six months until the police eventually got wind of these illegal parties and decided to bring a halt to proceedings, which they did, but not without a fight. By the time all parties had been stopped around the country, thousands of pounds worth of equipment had been seized and many people had been given jail sentences for their involvement.

It was time to make things legal, as this wasn't something that would go away overnight.

Delight

Sasha had already moved on and fortunately secured a residency at Bugsy's nightclub in Ashton. It was from here that his name would gain a certain magnitude that would only increase each time he played.

His success continued around the North West following a stint at a small sweat-inducing venue in Blackpool called Shaboo, where he cemented his reputation as THE DJ to be heard in the North. Due to its size, had you not gained access to the bar below by 8pm, there would be no guarantee of you gaining entrance to the club above, such was its popularity.

The surrounding car park would be rammed, with every available space filled, hence if you were the first one in parked in the far corner, you were the last one to leave. Every car blasted out there own bootleg copy of their favourite Sasha tape.

When the night came to a close, the car park was where you would try and persuade someone to let you borrow their prized tape, with a promise you would return it to them same time next week. The kind of persuasion needed would take the form of grovelling, pleading, begging and an array of sexual favours, such was the need to get hold of these soon to be pieces of history. This time was a realisation for many that the name of Sasha was a guarantee of a quality night.

i-D magazine had become something of a bible for us in the formative years of house music and with collaborators such as the Boys Own crew of Farley, Heller, Thatcher et al along with Oakenfold's Spectrum posse, if they said it was Christmas, then I was sat waiting for the Queen's speech. This was one of the best ways to find out which venues were to become tomorrow's 'Paradise Garage'. Both *i-D* and *Mixmag*, which was the only credible magazine at the time dedicated to dance music, had published rumours of a new night to be sought out in Staffordshire by the name of 'Delight', at a club called Shelley's. But even such established national publications could not beat the word from the 'street', and those in the know were already sampling the delights, pardon the pun, of this little known venue in Longton, near Stoke-on-Trent.

Fortunately, having frequented Shaboo on a weekly basis, I was well aware that the DJ making all the right noises was called Sasha and his next venture was Shelley's. Whispers inside and out of the Haçienda had been circulating since the closure of Shaboo and a small hardcore following were ready to take to the road once confirmation of his new residency had leaked out.

God is a DJ*

Sasha's decision to collaborate with good friend Gary McClarnan, a photographer for *Mixmag* at the time, was to mould the sound of things to come, and I recently asked the latter about the relationship he formed with the DJ which led to him becoming his first unofficial manager.

> *I lived in a house in Whalley Range with a guy called Morgan who was a hairdresser I got to know through a bunch of other people. I lived there around 1987, maybe even as early as 1986, he said. At the time I was taking photographs of the Haçienda and pretty much as a job, I was getting paid as a photographer. I was also working at Barge Format Camera Studios, shooting beer commercials at the same time as going out and doing the Haçienda on Tour.*

Gary's reputation led to a regular assignment at the Haçienda for each new night launched, and some of his most prestigious work ended up in the *Haçienda Must Be Built* book. During the period around 1987, Sasha was playing at pirate radio stations near where he lived in Old Trafford in a block of flats. By 1988, he and Gary acknowledged each other as regular faces at the Haç.

Sasha and Serena, his partner at the time, were desperate to find somewhere away from their current residence following continuous grief from their current landlord, and a vacancy at Gary's house had fortuitously become available.

> *A flat was available at ours, which was a pretty big house at the time, said Gary. We talked about it and Sasha moved in two weeks later. By that time Jon DaSilva had moved in upstairs where I lived so it was pretty much a public house. I had known Jon since he started working at the Haçienda DJing the 'Hot' nights on a Wednesday, and I met him through that.*

> *There was a kind of clique in the Haçienda from about 1985 through to 1989 which mainly revolved around Switch, who were the lighting guys, and also included Jon DaSilva, Graeme Park, Mike Pickering, Paul Cons who ran the Haç and Andy Berry who was Manchester's leading hairdresser. Anybody who was anybody, he did their hair.*

> *Everything was built around that kind of scene back then. There was a lot of hanging out at the Blackburn warehouse rave parties. I think at that point Sasha wasn't really being paid for DJing in any way. I remember there was £50 here and £100 there.*

Gary was an extremely resourceful person during this period, with an endless list of contacts through his photography and the circles he mixed in. At the same time he was plugging records as well as his good friend Sasha and offers of work came flooding in from all directions.

Mixmag had just started up as a fanzine and Gary was employed to provide some visual aspect to it.

> *I was asked to do some record plugging because I had a network of people I knew who were all DJs or performers and had just joined* Mixmag *when it was a DJ fanzine. At the same time I was taking photographs for the Boys Own fanzine and knew Terry Farley so I did cover features and stuff like that for Boys Own.* Mixmag *used to be a DJ fanzine that I started doing photographs for also. There was a guy called Nick Gordon-Brown and he, Dave Seaman and myself all kind of got together and made it into a style magazine. So I kind of spent a couple of years working for that as the staff photographer as well as DMC doing all the DMC tours. We had a mobile phone we shared around that time because we were getting calls in to do gigs and it made sense to have one.*

Having taken the rumours and a few lines of print in *Mixmag* and *i-D* magazine as gospel, I was determined and excited to see if the rumblings of a new residency for Sasha would be brought to fruition.

The first journey to a new club was always a night out in itself fraught with missed junctions and bad directions from all parties concerned, and on this particular night in September, 1990, there a general consensus that neither myself, Gareth or our other mate in the car, Dave, actually had any idea where Longton was. Maybe a map would have been of use but when you're young the road holds no fear and you're never lost in a car, or so my dad used to say.

After several trips past Stoke City Football Club and various signs for Alton Towers, we managed to pick one up for Hanley, which was close to its bigger brother Longton. We proceeded to drive round this quaint little town several times, pretending we were just getting the feel of the place, before we eventually found our target.

Shelley's Laserdome, to give it its full title, was from the outside was neither imposing nor inspiring, but it had its own car park in front of the doors, which incidentally would later be used in a publicity stunt by the gas mask-wearing Altern8 for their chart storming single *Activ8 (Come with Me)*. In these seminal months, the car park was actually used for cars but as the night picked up momentum over the next year it would be mainly occupied by around 2,000 young, ardent clubbers desperate to gain entry.

I still question how and why a little town called Longton in an obscure part of Staffordshire became such a phenomenon. Gary McClarnan tried to unravel the mystery behind it.

> *Prior to Shelley's, we tried a gig in either Widnes or Warrington, not sure where now, because we knew there was something out there. Nobody turned up, but we just thought that was because that was the wrong place to do it. We knew there was an interest in what he was doing.*

Gary locked onto Sasha's talents with a view to honing his ability to recognise what really moved a crowd enough for them to follow him wherever he played.

> *I knew Sasha was Grade 8 piano and although there were lots of people who were DJs with good record collections, there was something else about certain performers. He had the kind of talent to understand people. It's like he's enigmatic in his approach but a complete music head inside out. You know that's all people like him ever wake up and think about.*

The question was, where could they find a venue to showcase Sasha's sets and how far would people travel to hear him? But these were exciting times in clubland and no one was sure when this house music thing would die a death like the short-lived previous trends for New Romantic and punk music. Little did anyone realise how big a dent in music's historical sphere it would make. House music appeared to have no boundaries when it came to what lengths people would go to in order to listen to this new sound and more importantly their new heroes, so to speak. Whether they liked it or not, DJs were soon to replace the pop stars of yesteryear and it didn't matter where they played in the country, the crowd would follow.

By 1990, Gary had turned his hand to record plugging in addition to his photography and the overseeing of Sasha's DJ exploits.

The same time I stopped record plugging, I was asked by a friend to see this venue that needed to be turned round, he recalled. It was this rock venue in Stoke, which was on its arse. So I went down and had a look with him and his sidekick called Rick who used to drive a white XR3. I just walked in and thought 'This is it, this is the place.'

I'd been down there during the day to have a look and so went back in the evening to have another look. I went again for one last look a week later and it was full of Stoke City shirts, red and white, and it was awful. Maybe 200–300 people in there? This place at its height could hold 1,200 people. It was licensed I think at the time for about 900.

I said 'Yeh, I could do something with it,' and they said 'We're on our arse on a Friday and on Saturday so which one do you want?'

So I said 'I'll suck it and see and take the Fridays.' But at that point I'd never really promoted a night. I'd kind of done one-off gigs here and there but never really taken it on.

And so the aptly named 'Delight' at Shelley's was born. And it didn't take long to establish it as probably one of the best Friday nights in the history of dance music.

Travelling a distance was never an issue for me and close mates Gareth and Dave, the former who always had his ear to the ground be it a new night to go to or record released, and the latter who had always been more than happy to follow our lead and enjoy himself. And the fear of venturing into the unknown was one that clubbers in the early Nineties turned into the intrigue and attraction of finding a new place to party.

Gary never doubted that the masses would follow Sasha to the ends of the earth.

God is a DJ*

You can say, looking back in hindsight, 'What a cracking move'. But it was more a case of 'There's a venue. Can we get to it and back the same night and what are the issues?'

The thing that made it really magnetic was that within three or four weeks it was almost like a secret, because we'd promoted it quite well. We'd promoted it out to a leading influential group of people through our own network. We 'flyered' but kept it pretty low key. I think the best thing we did was give people exact instructions on how to get there from Manchester.

Ironically, people in the North West had always had a penchant for travelling distances in the search for great music to listen to, giving rise to the birth of Northern Soul in the Sixties, and 20 years later it had come full circle.

I think the first night we did about 350 people and it was a bit of a mix as well. The 350 were kind of people from around the North West, some from Blackburn, Manchester and Chester. People would come who had been travelling out to warehouse gigs and things like that. They kind of knew that doing 15–18 miles was a pretty regular thing and they might have been doing two or three venues a night.

So it was about 350 of our crowd and then another 100–150 of these Stoke City shirts. It went on for about three weeks and it was lifting each week. By the time the fourth or fifth week came around, the Haçienda was rumoured to be closing. We went from about 400 people to doubling within the next week. So easily within six weeks we were at capacity.

The club opened its doors at 9pm and closed shortly after the 2am curfew, never earlier, never later. After the first two months of opening, the car park had no room for cars due to the size of the queue of people who were arriving earlier by the week.

Unfortunately there were no guarantees of entry even after two hours' queuing, unless you managed to push your way in nearer the entrance. The cut-off point loomed for hundreds too polite to push in, but such is the British penchant for queuing, we stayed put and the result was often a long miserable drive home with thoughts of what might have been. I presume this incident must have occurred to the majority of regulars at the venue, but nevertheless this would only compound my determination to gain entry the following week. You would have thought an 8pm arrival would have ensured admission, but then again the other thousand or so regulars also had the same idea, such was the fervour to gain entry during this peak period.

The only other way to guarantee entry was the 'green card'. This encapsulated piece of card was the second most sought after item in clubland, behind a lock of Sasha's hair! It eliminated the worry of being waved away from the heaving entrance having salivated all week at work in anticipation of Friday night.

As Gareth worked for an advertising agency, he could produce a copy of the card down to the finest detail with no problem. The hardest task was getting an original to forge, but it was easier to complete a Rubik's Cube than get hold of one of these green treasures.

We finally managed to secure one on Delight's first birthday celebrations on 27th May 1991, which was a magical night from start to finish, as measured by the total weight of my sweat-soaked jeans and top, left on my bedroom floor without a dry patch on them. This was the point were parents start to worry as what you could possibly be doing that would produce so much perspiration. Not even a soak in the bath would make clothes that heavy.

Gareth made it his Monday morning priority to make three identical cards ready to be brandished at the door the following Friday. But unfortunately, that very week Sasha relinquished his residency. As with comedy, it's all about timing.

My first impression on the opening night at the Laserdome was of trepidation as I combed the room to find garish carpet, lots of chrome piping and decoration the likes of which reminded me of a Miami Vice set. It definitely had that Eighties glitz feel to it. You could almost hear Rick Astley giving you up.

But as I stood in my new red Ghostly Haberdasheries sweatshirt, hot from Affleck's Palace that afternoon, and sand coloured Kicker boots, still tainted with mud splashes from an industrial wasteland somewhere in Lancashire, the warming basslines cascading across the presently empty dance floor gave me instant amnesia with regards to the décor.

God is a DJ*

Sasha would usually play for the whole five hours but some weeks other commitments would take precedence and he would use the local lad Rick to play the first two hours.

Another of the warm up DJs was an unknown up and coming bloke going by the same name as a certain ex-England and Arsenal goalkeeper and with a ponytail to match. Now noted for his smooth bald looks Dave Seaman, later of Brothers in Rhythm and Renaissance fame, had the envious but difficult task of having to suppress any emotions spilling from eager clubbers wanting to make the most of their night out. His sets were sound odysseys that crept towards their gentle climaxes with gorgeous precision, leaving everyone more than satisfied with the beats per minute.

A lot of Dave's production and playlist would have a large influence on the career path of new resident Sasha. Together they would champion the screaming Italian vocal sets that were now the toast of northern clubbing.

Any Sasha set that had been recorded at the time became the most sought after bootleg tape around the country. If you were fortunate enough to get a copy, or rather a tape that had probably already been copied a thousand times, such was the sound quality of such bootlegs, woe betide you if you ever let it out of your grasp/car/home, as you probably wouldn't see it again.

A steady train of similarly dressed baggy clubbers streamed into the now half-filled venue with a smattering already taking their positions on the dancefloor. A few we presumed were close friends of Sasha and Gary as they emitted a glow of confidence in what seemed like their own personal dancing space.

We, on the other hand, held our position near the bar, facing the shiny chrome DJ booth, each displaying our own pensive motions in time to the slowly building tempo of the music.

The lighting system began increasing its cycle of dazzling effects, establishing why it had taken the name 'Laserdome'. As the spray of flat, green light emitted from the far corner of the venue, cutting into the masses on the now swarming dancefloor, the BPM's had increased noticeably. This was evident as I found I was now positioned quite a distance from the bar and stood on the periphery of the chaos that was about to unfold in front of me.

Listening to tapes in the car entitled 'Sasha 15 Oct 1990' when I'm having a nostalgic moment to myself, the tempo of his sets from this era seems almost ambient compared to subsequent house music, such did the pace of the music increase during the next decade. But hasn't everything speeded up during the last 15 years or so, or is it that I'm slowing down?

As I looked up towards the DJ booth straight opposite me, I could clearly see the white shirted, trademark ponytailed figure of Sasha. With an intense expression etched on his face, he prepared to impart his night's concoction of screaming female vocals and massive piano breaks onto a crowd now at the mercy of his cross fader. His now much publicised long, swirling intros, that had become his forte during these formative years, were beginning to control the floor like a snake charmer.

The Orb's 10 minute remix of Erasure's *Ship of Fools* with its floating, haunting build up still gives me goose bumps to this day. Tracks like this set the tone for the night and emotions began to build as Sasha teased us with breaks and a cappellas before unleashing tracks such as *Cartouche*, *Hi Liner* and *Appolonia* that left you so elated you could burst.

Such banging Italian anthems with their big piano breakdowns had a real innocent energy to them. So many of the records played have come to be regarded as Shelley's classics. Each person probably has their own favourite which they have subsequently bored their younger contemporaries with how as to massive a track it was and the emotional effect it brought to the dancefloor.

This was a time when, all things being new, records now regarded as classics were played and made every Friday, and Sasha knew this only too well. Along with all that was good coming out of Italy with its penchant for piano breaks and massive female vocals, he would intersperse these screaming anthems with tracks you wouldn't have dreamed he'd be able to get away with playing.

New Years Eve 1990 was one such instance. Tickets had sold out within two weeks of going on sale. For the regulars there was nowhere else you wanted to be even if it had been offered to you for free. This particular night remains my best New Year's Eve to date, physically draining yet so emotionally uplifting I was close to tears and didn't want the night to end.

The variety of tracks played during this period was something I don't think Sasha deliberately sought to do.

God is a DJ*

I was just mixing it up, he said. There were a lot of big, happy Italian records out at the time, and the Haçienda's music policy had changed to where they were playing a lot of American house.

I think I was one of the first people to be banging about those big, big, happy records and whipping the crowd up into a real kind of mental frenzy. It really did go off in there, people had their tops off and had air horns and whistles. It was amazing.

Most of the time I used to DJ the whole night, and I would push it every week to see how late I could take it before I played a record that they knew. I knew that by the time I played the first record they knew, I would have to leather the sound to keep the energy level at the highest.

I used to play the most obscure records. I played a lot of tunes from the Big Shot label in Canada and really deep sounds, but as soon as they recognised one sound in a record, that was it. The whole place would go right off, and I would kind of have to play that big sound the rest of the night.

The ability to be able to play and get away with tracks such as Bruce Hornsby's *The Way It Is* and James Ingram's *Yah Mo B There* confirmed Sasha to me as some kind of magician. Tracks like these were good on their own merits but when fused with house anthems of the time I can only try conveying to people the feeling of utopia. Obviously for many, Ecstasy had a lot to do with it, the drug of choice at the time being definitely a major contributing factor to state of euphoria in the place.

When I tell my friend Warby, who is the resident DJ for my own night, of these tracks that Sasha played, he just looks at me in disbelief. In 2003, when hosting our own Ace of Clubs party upstairs in Sankeys Soap, Manchester, the last record Warby played after security had cleared everyone downstairs was Bruce Hornsby's classic, leaving myself and Gareth going mad in the middle of an empty dancefloor to a true Shelley's moment. Such tracks transported your soul to a place of awe-inspiring happiness. People visibly glowed with a look of enchantment.

One person I remember in particular was Nicola Stephenson who played Margaret in Brookside. You know the one who had the kiss with Anna Friel. She was one of the many regular faces at most of the early, influential house nights around the North West at venues such as Legends in Warrington and the Haçienda.

I can picture her now stood on the edge of the dancefloor with a beaming grin and flushed cheeks as the vociferous tones of *Such a Good Feeling* by Brothers in Rhythm was unleashed in full effect, miming every word in unison along with the rest of the club. This track was written by Dave Seaman and his production partner Steve Osbourne specifically for Shelley's and epitomised the emotion felt by everyone who passed through the doors.

As each Friday built up, from leaving work that evening to arriving at the club, the expectancy for the master to perform increased each week. Gary summed up the euphoria that surrounded the club and the ethos behind its success in addition of course to the ubiquitous Sasha.

> *That anticipation in the queue and the curtailment of a night were really, really important, he said.*
>
> *After the seventh or eighth week, driving there and being there at half past six and seeing a massive queue, I remember thinking this is phenomenal and just really, really enjoying it, going up and down the queue and bumping into a few friends and faces. They would be really friendly so it was almost as though it was a real fraternity.*

The anticipation of getting in, coupled with the charged atmosphere, made it a special place to be. The crowd would be baying for a massive stab of emotion to be unleashed from the PA system and could only be held back for so long.

Sasha tried to explain to Sheryl Garrett in her wonderful book, *Adventures in Wonderland*, the rigours of controlling such a thirsty crowd.

> *The big thing for me was holding the crowd back, he said. They'd be gagging to hear a record they knew and as soon as they did, the whole place would go mental. From that point onwards I knew I had to completely go for it. As soon as I put that one record on, the air horns would go off and that would be it. I'd have to completely hammer it.*

God is a DJ*

My most vivid memory is the moment when the first raptures of PKA's *Temperatures Rising* emitted from the speakers to an instant hands in the air ovation from all and sundry, including the bar staff. As the first bars of the track broke, the air horns sounded and lights responded in perfect motion to reveal glistening faces, perspiring in the heat-soaked atmosphere which ironically mirrored the aforementioned track. You'd think the track, more of which we will hear of later, was written with Shelley's in mind. However so many other clubs up and down the country, with Hacketts in Blackpool and Quadrant Park in Liverpool instantly springing to mind, had the same fog-like mist of condensation forming from sweat drenched clubbers.

A change of clothes was as necessary to the car boot as a spare wheel and jack if you wanted to avoid that uncomfortable car journey home. That included underwear and a fresh pair of jeans as these were usually soaked to the knee, such was the intense heat of the venue. Your de rigueur cotton long-sleeved top could be wrung out as it was drenched in your own sweat as well as that of a few topless morons who continued to brush past you throughout the evening.

To the back of the club, a huge cooling vent was employed along with the standard air conditioning vents, yet only those in its immediate vicinity could feel any benefit whatsoever. My regular spot was near neither so I was just left to sweat it out, but who cared when the music was so good?

Everything worked in harmony and Gary pointed out to me why it worked so well.

You had the three aspects, the queue, Sasha and the intensity of the night, he said.

Sasha was playing all night but in addition to these elements, through my contacts, I started to get live acts like Sharmoni and Alison Limerick, Two for Joy and Orbital and various people to play unannounced. Halfway through the night they'd come on and play, which I remember lots of times really, really made the night.

Some nights we wouldn't do it and just have Sasha playing all night and that would build a kind of anticipation within the gig. Then I remember we had Sharmoni over who had done that Peace in the Valley track and we just got her to start singing from the back of the club. People thought it was just the track playing and it was actually her. Then she walked through the back of the club and stood on one of the podiums and people went mental.

There would be no containing the crowd who were now in full flow and so Sasha could do nothing else but, to coin a phrase, 'take you higher', and this he did, probably too well.

To add weight to the music and atmosphere Gary finally got the owners to fix the laser from which the club attained its name.

The laser hadn't worked for years and I kept getting on to them to get it repaired, so the first time the laser worked we hadn't told anybody and just switched it on. The reaction was absolutely mental.

Lasers back then were really dodgy and a bit hit and miss. It would work for four weeks and then die. It would take another two months to find a laser engineer who would come and fix it. Again we wouldn't tell anybody it was fixed and just switch it on half way through the night.

As two o'clock approached with what always seemed like the speed of 10 ravers, it would be clear that neither the crowd nor Sasha wanted to leave the venue or stop the music. In these early hedonistic days, a two o'clock curfew was the norm but such was the passion Sasha pledged to these special Friday nights the last record would usually sneak past the witching hour, much to the disgust of the security who would wave a menacing, solitary finger indicating 'the last one'.

With images of euphoria seared onto our consciousness, the night had to end somewhere, but people weren't ready to go home yet. The only places open at such an early hour were the service stations and the preferred choice of the Shelley's regulars happened to be Knutsford. Fortunately for us that was on the way home, which was nice!

Had we had a bit of foresight, my Rizla stall would now be an empire such was the popularity of the daddy of all papers. If I'd have sold each pack for a solitary pound during this boom time then who knows where I would have ended up today?

God is a DJ*

Knutsford Services was a place where people chilled, smoked, laughed and swapped those now legendary Shelley's tapes that are currently on most auction sites on the net for about 15 quid apiece. Its popularity over the next six months meant turnover increased 20 fold, much to the delight of the manager. But as with most large gatherings, petty crime and security became an issue. Soon after, the police cordoned off the slip road on both sides of the motorway to prevent access to the service area at that was the end of that. Gary recalled that very night.

> I remember that night they closed Knutsford Services and wouldn't let us in. Dave Seaman needed petrol. He reversed up the ramp and got caught. We'd gone to the next services at Keele and waited for him. In the end everyone ended up going to Keele and they loved it.

> When Knutsford first happened, 200 people were there the first night, then 400 constantly. The manager loved us and became our best mate. We'd come in saying 'Expect whole bunch of people'. But after a while people started taking the piss and taking things and turning the music up really loud. People coming in wanting a break from driving up the M6 couldn't get a break.

Sasha's residency was very short lived, with his first set in September 1990 and his last set nostalgically being Delight's first birthday celebrations on 27th May 1991. There was gridlock from as early as 8pm that night as the little town of Longton came to a standstill.

Queues were of epic proportions as everyone clambered to get as near to the door as possible even though it was a ticket event. The night felt like a New Year's Eve and expectations were surpassed with ease as another extraordinary night came to a premature end for everyone present. Nobody knew this was going to be Sasha's last appearance but every time he played here it felt like it was the last party on earth, such was the intensity of the nights.

Sasha was becoming more and more in demand from other promoters around the world and his feeling for the club had started to wane. The partying that went on during that particular year was relentless with no day of rest and signs of excess were beginning to show on all concerned, in particular Sasha and Gary, who had partied harder than most.

We'd be doing Shelley's on Fridays, Kicks and the Eclipse in Coventry on Saturdays, Time in Birmingham, maybe a few warehouse parties, then we'd do Park Hall every other Thursday, recalled Gary.

About that time the gigs would start Wednesday and by Sunday morning, we'd come out of Coventry about 8am and we'd all be wasted. I'd drive then and we'd probably go to Geoff Oakes' house and then spend until Monday or Tuesday there then a day recovering, then go back out on the Wednesday. This just kept happening.

Geoff had a little house in Biddulph. Back then he wasn't a promoter, he was just a man about Stoke really and actually he was very helpful and resourceful. Whenever you needed something he would help out.

He had connections and was getting more and more into music at the time. You could see him wanting to be a promoter, booking DJs etc. It was really obvious that was going to happen but it's easier for me to say this now than at the time.

Sunday morning would be recovery time and if it wasn't at Geoff's house it would be at Sasha's house. Monday was trying to get back together again to keep going. We'd start again on Wednesday, spend most of our money on drugs, do 2,000 miles in a week and be wasted. I was still taking photographs at the time, going to London for a couple of days and coming back up north for the weekend.

During those halcyon days, the success of Shelley's meant that along with the football it was very much at the forefront of Stoke's weekend agenda.

But this brought with it the unwanted attention of the local council and Staffordshire Police who were keen to ensure nothing underhand or illegal was occurring. Obviously where there's a successful club in any town or city, there's a thriving drug scene, and where there's drugs, there's money.

God is a DJ*

Shelley's was just out of control in a way, said Gary. Not in a bad way, just that I had to renegotiate my deal.

The week after I came back, we had Moss Side trying to take the door takings the night I was on the door. It was pretty full on and got really intense. One of the guys there got a hatchet in the knee.

We then had to move the team that were on the door from a Stoke team to a Birmingham team. It was my job to manage all that end, as well as the guy who owned the venue and the venue manager. It was a pretty intense time.

Surveillance teams were quickly set up to monitor the comings and goings and the police were also keen to establish whether overcrowding was also occurring in the rammed to capacity club. Gary knew it was only a matter of time before he would be challenged on this count.

We had been taken to court as we were letting 1,200 people in. The guy that owned the venue wanted people in and we wanted people in to experience it. There may have been a sense of greediness in making sure everybody could get in but we were still turning enough away enough to fill a sports hall across the way which was playing a similar kind of music. You could walk to it round the corner but it was awful.

Soon after it started up I walked in with Geoff Oakes and someone else. They were shitting themselves that we were going to take it over. That wasn't us, we just left it. But they had found inefficiency in us and exploited it.

The police then got really heavy and we had the restriction down to 700 people, so were turning even more people away. The place felt quite empty but it was still buzzing and people really appreciated getting in there.

But what was happening was the old crowd couldn't get in and the new crowd were getting there at 5.30 and getting in so we were losing touch with the original people. In a sense the club from lots of different angles had had its day. It drifts for a while and you have to know the end point. At the time we should have moved it on.

Sasha's popularity at Shelley's had spread sooner than we all probably wanted it to. In an ideal world it would have been nice to keep the night a secret for six months longer, then maybe his residency would have continued past the first birthday.

However this wasn't to be, and being part of the original crowd we were now struggling to gain entry even though we were arriving two hours earlier than our previous arrival time. So we started to make it only a monthly venture instead of weekly pilgrimage, spending the other three Fridays of the month at our much nearer Haçienda, charmed by Mike Pickering's 'Shine' night. Ironically, Sasha would end up DJing as a regular guest of Mike's when not playing at Delight at Shelley's, much to our own delight.

Gary's realistic perceptions of Shelley's were his saving grace in the end, and he timed his exit to perfection.

There was a downward slope towards the end of 1991, and I came back after six weeks out in November 1991 and said 'This is the end of this.' I had gone to the club a couple of times and thought 'This isn't it, not what it was.'

But we did New Year and it was fantastic, like the reigniting of something. We got more people in than the 700 capacity, went to court and disputed their counting as they'd been using two or three cameras. We said they'd been counting everyone twice and the court believed it so the police had to drop the case.

We nudged it up to 950 then 1,000 again. New Year was such a fantastic gig that we decided to run for another two months and then close. We couldn't trust anyone else to do it so said to the owners 'It's up to you what do with venue, there's nothing left here for us anymore,' and so it died on its arse. The last ever night I did had a really good line up. It was really enjoyable and then that was it.

With the world now at his feet, Sasha took his box of delights and ponytail to pastures new.

Shelley's promoters tried to resurrect the night, calling it 'Tootie Frootie' with the DJ baton in the capable hands of resident Dave

Seaman. Prestigious guest DJ line-ups included the likes of Laurent Garnier and Frankie Knuckles, but there was only one way the club could go following the departure of 'the man-like', as many of us called Sasha, and today it no longer stands. The old car park is full of shoppers, with the club now converted to another great British institution – a Lidl supermarket!

One particular nostalgic Sunday last year, I played about four Shelley's tapes in succession, fitting in perfectly to a Sunday afternoon after Hollyoaks, which yes, I watch too. After the fourth tape faded out and clicked off, I decided to send a text message to Sasha, something along the lines of 'Oct 1990, most emotional tape ever. Shelley's was the place to be and luckily I was there! Thanks for the memories!'

Moments later my phone rang. I looked at the screen to see who dared interrupt my blissful Sunday. 'Be a bird,' I thought. But no, it was the man himself asking if I could send some copies down to him. A refreshing change for me to be making tapes for him.

2

Solstice

Manchester Academy, July 1991

THE heady days of '91 and big piano anthems were most definitely my bag.

Summer had arrived early and was looking like it was going to stay with us until the Indian one in September.

Short sleeves and white were the two staple requirements as regards dress sense went, but still anything with everything was the order of the day. Dress codes on flyers were rarely taken much note of during the early years of house music as each part of the country had their own style.

London was just getting all black and biker style with a lot of designer labels coming to prominence like John Richmond's 'Destroy' and Michiko Koshino, whereas Manchester was still baggy and colourful thanks to Kickers, Wallabee's and Chipie to name a few.

How times have changed, with some of the so called exclusive clubs up and down the country now employing door pickers on a weekly basis to sift out whether or not your look is right for their night.

This is where the pretentiousness and snobbery of people kicks in, though it has proved to be a very effective marketing tool in all major cities in the UK, particularly where bar culture has threatened to bypass club culture due to the revised late licensing laws. The more exclusive a bar becomes the more people clamour to get in. I suppose that just proves the stature to which dance music has progressed and the way it has dominated this field over the years.

Sasha by this time had moved out of Gary McClarnan's house, split with his girlfriend and moved into a three-storey town house on Fire Station Square in Salford, close to Manchester city centre. With best mate Sparrow for company and new girlfriend Marie, his time in the flat was mainly spent recovering from the night's excesses.

Travelling around 2,000 miles a week, courtesy of Gary and his car, was beginning to take its toll as Gary explained to me.

God is a DJ*

There was a time about November 1991 when everything was just falling apart. Then I think it was that Christmas that was the killer. The most annoying thing was that hanging out at Sasha's house was becoming the de riguour thing for everyone.

What I tended to do was go out and get vitamins and stuff like that to get rid of mouth ulcers. We were bad, my hair was falling out and I couldn't sleep. We were killing ourselves at the time. I was trying to find as many recovery solutions as I could do, as managers do. Even though I wasn't a formal manager, I was doing all the jobs that a manager does.

In between convalescing in time for the next gig, Sasha was frequently being asked to remix tracks for artists such as Annie Lennox as well as local dance outfit Evolution, for whom he did his first ever remix.

Gary's earlier record plugging days had paid off big time as he had a list of contacts with all the major and independent record labels, but the situation was beginning to stretch his capabilities as a manager-cum-fixer.

I didn't know what a manager was, he said. We stopped working together as I didn't know enough about the music industry, the legal and business side.

I took him down to do his first remixes but we were being walked all over by the music industry. Sasha's first mixes or attempts at doing remixes were for DMC through connections with AVL which was a Virgin label at the time. The first remix he did that came out was on Ten records through a guy called Rob Manley who was working at Virgin. It was a very early one, it really didn't go anywhere.

I remember at the time Sasha was just getting his head round technology so he was going into the studio and at the same time we were doing the gigs at the weekend and then going down to London to DMC for a few days, coming back up for Wednesday/Thursdays. We were doing even more miles back then. I don't think I was doing any photography at that time.

Ibiza was experiencing its fifth 'Summer of Love' since Paul Oakenfold, Danny Rampling and Nicky Holloway had returned to our shores with tales of a Balearic nirvana. The demand for British DJs to play out there had increased each year, probably thanks to the likes of Alex P and Brandon Block who were living there full time. Sasha went over a couple of times in 1991 with mates Sparrow, Gary and local DJ Pigsy.

The partying though had started to outweigh the playing time and on their return, the darker side of clubland had surfaced on his own doorstep. Gary recalls an incident that changed Sasha's outlook on the people that he was now surrounded by.

It was probably about Christmas/New Year 1991 at Sasha's house in Salford. We discovered that money had been stolen from his bedroom, a lot of money from three or four gigs over that Christmas period.

It was a really warm environment hanging out at Sasha's house up to that point, but he wouldn't let people come round for a bit after that. Everyone had suspicions and nobody really trusted anyone any more.

I remember sitting down with Sasha and he said: 'At least I know it wasn't you,' but that wasn't really helping as there was another 12 to 15 people here. When you're in some kind of nirvana, that tarnish doesn't go away unless you eradicate everybody and then lose the cohort of people in the first place. That was a pretty intense time.

Sasha continued to thrive with his DJing and the demand for his input for remixes and production work increased each month, but the weekly parties held at his house had gone. No longer could he freely invite whoever he liked back for fear of someone taking advantage of a unique situation.

Gary had realised that times were changing in both of their lives.

The deterioration happened all the way through 1991 and from September of that year things had pretty much ended. For me certainly, it had come to an end, the warmth and enjoyment of it all. I'm a business person now but I wasn't then. I was enjoying the culture in the same way any hip hop or rave kid would, but I had the opportunity to get beyond the velvet rope more often than anyone else because of my contacts. I was never a drug

God is a DJ*

dealer and neither was Sasha which was quite unique amongst those kinds of people. You had segments of people, those who bombed it at the weekends and worked all week, and the ones who kind of bummed around all the time and were at every gig, scrimping and saving, flogging drugs and Chipie shirts to try and keep themselves going out.

Fortunately both Sasha and Gary realised they had reached saturation point and would need to take their foot off or self-destruct. That happened only a few months after the point when Sasha had been elevated to a status unbeknown to any previous DJ in the UK, and that included Jimmy Savile!

In New York during the Seventies disco phenomenon, DJs had reached a pinnacle of their powers and were hugely influential to the point of dictating to the masses how people dressed, how they walked, who to be seen with and where to go. Clubs like the Gallery, the Loft, Studio 54 and Paradise Garage had more influence on a city than anything that had gone before. Tim Lawrence's educational book *Love Saves The Day* gives a fantastic account of how powerful DJs became during this boom period from 1970 to 1979, but I believe the UK never caught onto such a phenomenon until the summer of 1991.

Sasha, playing in his adopted hometown, was guaranteed to fill wherever he was booked to play, but with a new venue for us to visit at the Manchester Academy, expectations were mixed. The Academy is situated in the heart of 'studentville', a short distance away from the bustling centre of Manchester, and there was bound to be a surprise element as to the kind of crowd it would attract aside from his faithful following. The purpose built venue mainly held gigs for all the major bands touring the country, so to have a DJ play there, not as a warm up to a band but as the main act, was something new.

Years later, I was lucky to see the legendary Leftfield here, promoting their 'Rhythm and Stealth' album, and the award winning Guinness ad track *Phat Planet* is still etched in my mind to this day, such was the ferocity of noise that emitted from the sound system. This colossal wall of speakers was transported around the country with them, and added to two 30 foot high visual screens that filled the stage, it mirrored the actual advert of crashing ocean waves and thundering white stallions. I still have a hoof mark as proof.

Demand for tickets for Sasha had been increasing for a good three months prior to the event before eventually selling out well in advance, such was the fervour generated. Very little promotion was needed in the way of flyers, billboards or national press. In any case, these were early days for such promotional activity and with *Mixmag* being the only dance dedicated publication at the time, word of mouth more than anything was king. And from the melee that formed outside the venue beforehand it became clear that a lot of people had been talking.

The promoters were obviously not expecting the demand to obtain entry to resemble scenes from a Beatles concert. Crash barriers had been strategically placed along the line of the building to ensure some sort of regulation and as this was an all ticket affair, you would have presumed everybody was guaranteed entry.

But as the crowd swelled and barriers came down, all sorts of pandemonium was awry. The temperature outside the venue was what could be described as uncomfortably warm, yet compared to the crush we were about to experience once in the queue, the conditions could be considered tranquil.

People were clambering to get in as soon as physically possible. This was Sasha-mania now in full flow as people started to faint, get irritated, squashed and eventually pissed off with the whole shambles that was unfolding in front of us. By a stroke of luck and copious amounts of pushing, the crowd I had ventured out with managed to stay together and after a good hour or so of mayhem, we were at the door with ticket in hand. Some of us were now eager to gain entry with others just glad they had made it that far.

Once inside, we headed straight for the bar area just outside the main arena for a few swift looseners. The familiar sounds of DSK's *What Would We Do?* emanated from the booming PA system that filled the place with the same effect of wearing headphones, such was the intensity of noise.

Hashin's *Al Naafiysh*, an electro track from 1982, was one of Sasha's many surprise tracks from the night, showing the diversity in the music he played at the time, be it house, disco, electro or techno. To us it was just fantastic music. As clubbers filed into to the venue at an alarming rate to negate the crush that I presumed was continuing outside, capacity was reaching a satiated point before our eyes.

God is a DJ*

After a short but bustling journey into the main room, we entered to a large cheer from the heaving throng, maybe to mark our arrival I thought, as we were part of the Sasha faithful after all. But no, the reaction was sparked by the sound of *Karina's Temptation* spilling out over the crowd, who were now moving in unison and joining in the chorus of what has become one of those many Sasha classics included in record catalogues dotted around the country.

Some of the tracks listed in these mini bibles I never remember Sasha playing and more to the point I've never even heard of. I know I wasn't present everywhere he played and I don't have an 'audiophonic' memory, but if there was a big track I was aware he was caning at the time, then I'd be the biggest anorak around, going to any lengths to get hold of a copy.

I presume all those tracks listed have a piano theme to them followed by the words 'Sasha Classic'. With those words following them, even baked beans would more than likely increase sales, so who am I to argue?

As I skimmed the now swarming venue for the best spot to sustain the night ie not too far from the DJ, a speaker and the bar, I caught sight of Sasha aloft above the nearest watering hole, where the decks had been stationed. This elevated status was the epitome of DJ heaven I presumed, enabling the crowd and Sasha to interact between each other.

Dressed in a white, short sleeved T-shirt, locked into his headphones with his usual staid expression etched on his face, he began to control the crowd, as was his wont. The atmosphere, after all the animosity that had gone on outside, was one of pleasure and delight. People around me began to smile profusely, realising they were hearing something very special indeed and honoured to be in the presence of the 'man like' and his concoction of vinyl.

Arms reached for the skies yet again when the instantly recognisable piano-led intro to SLD's *Getting Out* came to the fore. There was now no going back and the hook line in the chorus rang out so true: 'Get ready for the best night of your life'.

There will always be tracks that everyone knows and loves but only a chosen few have access to.

Today's music scene has been taken over by the digital revolution with accessibility becoming easier by the day thanks to the downloading phenomenon via the internet. Even the pop charts sales figures now include downloads in the totals.

Unfortunately in 1991, dance music's only accessible formats to the public came in the form of vinyl or a tape/cassette, as even CDs were very much a third form of audio sales.

Sasha was already renowned from his Shelley's days for playing records that would only be available to Joe Public in 12 months' time. From experience, the more elusive a record, the more you ached to hear it played out. Two such tracks at the time, Zoë's *Sunshine on a Rainy Day* and K-Klass's *Rhythm is a Mystery* were virtually unattainable and the only chance you got to hear them would be when they were played by him. The aching could be felt all around like in a dentist's waiting room as we were teased and tantalised by the hypnotic sounds that Sasha poured through the immense PA system. Short stabs of the aforementioned records were injected into his set over the next four or five tracks that ensured the atmosphere was taken up a notch.

Now that Sasha had hypnotised everyone with his trademark long, swirling intros, stonking pianos and wailing female vocals, we were now in the palm of his hand. His ability to control a crowd had always impressed me no matter where he was playing or who he was playing to. Even in such a short space of time during these early years, I appreciated his gift to be able to restrain, lift and dictate to the crowd where he wanted them to be at any given time during his performances. Myself, and I presume thousands like me, were only too happy to be carried along by such uplifting sounds.

The tempo then noticeably dropped down a few beats per minute, combining Italo-esque synths with sunset-laden guitar licks that flowed beautifully into Zoë's summer anthem *Sunshine on a Rainy Day* which was then given its full airing, her vocals drifted over the baying crowd as if an invisible mist had landed on them. Whistles of the referees' variety began to shriek above the PA system as smiles adorned the longing faces of such a young crowd, mine included. This was the track we had been waiting for. And just when you thought emotions couldn't run any higher, the sound of local boys K-Klass's massive *Rhythm is a Mystery* broke out from nowhere. The place went mental and Sasha's face beamed with delight at the reaction he had created.

God is a DJ*

But this was Sasha and his genius was in playing two versions of the record simultaneously so not only did you get the chorus repeating itself, but also the emotions lasting twice as long. As Paul Daniels used to say, 'That's magic!'

Had Sasha played for the next eight hours in the same vein, nobody would have moved from their spot, but as it was the encore that wasn't possible. However, it still lasted for half an hour after the 2am curfew, much to the disgust of the surly bouncers who could be seen issuing stern instructions from below the booth that no more records could be played.

The crowd though, still hypnotised, refused to move. The stamping of feet and increasing handclap of defiance left the mercurial one with no option but to play on. But it was only for the length of an intro before security literally pulled the plug.

Boos and whistles resonated around the Academy as the noise level reached football match proportions, such was the disappointment of crowd, who clearly had a good few hours left in them. Yet the boos suddenly turned into a rapturous appreciation of a now confirmed superstar DJ, whether he liked the title or not. As he took his well earned adulation from his pulpit above the crowd, which was still showing no signs of dispersing, Sasha had a look of bewilderment at how well he had been received.

However a hint of slight embarrassment then came across his young but quickly maturing brow. Suddenly, from nowhere, a distinctive head of blond hair appeared in front of Sasha, arms aloft. To our astonishment it was an old school friend of mine called John Heron, who had travelled down separately on the off chance of picking up a ticket from one of the touts outside. Now he was having his finest moment, lapping up the adulation in front of probably 2,000 people all wishing it was them. I know I did.

As we were ushered out of the venue by the now disgruntled security, people wore their own inimitable smile. It was impossible for anyone's mood to be blackened such was the euphoria with which people exited.

I distinctly remember the night air hitting my sodden white T-shirt, and I wondered to myself if we really had witnessed what *Mixmag* were soon to highlight in the coming months – The 'Son of God'?

3

Haçienda Night

Ministry of Sound, London, June 1992

AT 21 years old, I don't think there's another time in your life when you are more up for new nights, new cities and most excitingly for me, new venues.

It was 1992, and 'super-clubs' reigned the clubbing highways in this boom period, but despite the Haçienda being probably most globally recognised brand on the market, such super clubs were a new venture for myself and most Haç regulars.

Yet whether you were Friday night 'Shine' goers or pledged your allegiance to Graeme Park on the Saturday, the lure of taking the Manchester vibe to one such super club, London's own Ministry of Sound, was as good as it got without getting on a plane to the 'White Island' of Ibiza. The little fact that the name Sasha had also been added to the roster to represent the northern quarter meant we would have quite a significant presence in the South for one night at least.

Around this time, people in the South seemed very sceptical of the Sasha legend as they already had their own DJ icons in Oakenfold, Cox, and Rampling. How could someone from the North be doing things bigger and better than what they already had?

Any time Sasha played a gig south of the border, at places like Boys Own or Shave yer Tongue for example, the feedback always seemed to be mixed, people being reluctant to give him the adulation he received back home.

> They wouldn't take me seriously, Sasha told Muzik's Andy Crysell.

> It wasn't until James Baillie of Venus, Nottingham took my mix tapes to people like Charlie Chester and Terry Farley, of Flying and Boys Own records respectively, without telling them who I was, that they decided they loved what I was doing and to book me.

God is a DJ*

I blame the smog for not letting his magic dust settle sooner on the South, but having spoken to him various times on this matter, I learned this only increased his determination to prove his doubters wrong, though for a time it did dent his confidence somewhat.

There was a buzz around the Haçienda in the weeks that preceded the Ministry weekend. Everyone exiting the venue after another hard Friday night's dancing was asking:

Who you going down with? Are ya staying over? What ya wearing? Have you been before?"

Excited at the prospect of going down to the 'Big Smoke' for the first time, let alone Ministry of Sound, people hung around outside the 'Haç' for a good hour afterwards confirming travel arrangements. These were pre-mobile phone days, where if you missed someone that was it, you never saw them unless you fortunately bumped into them inside the club, but the size of Ministry would make this highly unlikely. I think things were just a lot slower before mobiles became attached to our sides, and people were far more patient. Whether that's a good thing or not is another argument altogether, but speaking for today's clubbing climate, the mobile phone seems as essential as a sound system.

We had decided to hire a car for the weekend as I was travelling to Newcastle the following day with a different set of mates for a 21st birthday do. The cost split between nine was minimal and the fact that my good friend Julia, a Shelley's regular incidentally, was working at Salford Van Hire at the time, meant it was an even better deal than a 99p Burger King promotion. Armed with two Sasha tapes from October '90 and January '91 respectively and a Graeme Park one from March '91 for the car stereo, the journey down seemed to pass in a flash with so much excited banter, bad gags and getting lost.

This was standard practice for friends Gareth, Dave and I whenever we set out to find a new venue anywhere in the country. No matter which one of us drove, we could locate the vicinity of the place without any fuss, but finding the actual venue always proved elusive. We once did 30 circuits at least of Nottingham city centre trying to find an after-party we'd been given tickets for by James Baillie from Venus. In the end we just drove home in broad daylight with thoughts of what might have been, but if you're ever struggling to find Lower Regent St in Nottingham just give me a call!

Haçienda Night

Picking up the signs for Elephant & Castle, we knew our destination was not far from our reach and it was only 9pm, so we even had time to miss another turning or two. I remember parking not being a problem despite horror stories you would hear from people saying they'd never take a car south of Watford Gap again, and no sooner had we locked the doors when we bumped into friends not four car spaces away. Who needs mobile phones eh?

The queue was quite substantial by this time but that was a good sign and we had tickets so there were, so we hoped, no worries of not gaining entrance, unlike the Haçienda around that time where even sleeping with the owner didn't guarantee you entrance. So I'm told anyway.

The 10-feet-high iron gates that surrounded the entrance seemed pretty daunting at first, giving off a fortress-like feeling. Whereas in Manchester we were experiencing difficulties at various nights around that time with gangsters and ram-raiders, we presumed that in London the trouble element was that bit more heavy duty, hence the need for the iron curtain. As you may have noticed, the gates are so synonymous with the club that they have been used as the backdrop to the club logo, which is now recognised globally like the golden arches of McDonalds.

On entering the club, the imposing flyer that adorned the adjacent wall had the name 'SASHA' headlining the event with Mr Park's name in a slightly less commanding size of font. Nonetheless, I noticed the salient effect on all that entered as people handed over their ticket, turned away from the booth and looked the flyer up and down as if it were an attractive member of the opposite sex.

The club consisted of just two rooms during this period, the back room being split into two levels whilst also boasting the longest bar in Europe. That didn't mean it was any easier to get served, even though the bar staff were each provided with a pair of Nikes to speed up service between punters.

Graeme Park had already taken to the decks in the bar area giving his best Haçienda impression with Solution's *Feel So Right* and the massive Robin S track *Show Me Love* being lapped up by the Saturday night regulars.

People had begun to make the bar their podium for the night and this was before midnight. A good sign if ever there was one. Familiar faces were strewn around the bar now which was in full Haçienda

God is a DJ*

motion. People sang along to their favourites while others were just getting lost in the music.

Whilst trying to find a good vantage point, you couldn't help bumping into friends with alarming regularity as everyone in the room seemed to be from Manchester. It felt like those moments on holiday when you bump into someone from home in the middle of a Spanish nightclub. Everybody seemed to be all hugs and kisses as if they were long lost schoolmates, and yet it was only the previous weekend they'd seen them in the Haçienda and not even spoke to each other. Must have been that 'Big Smoke' they all talk about? All this commotion and Sasha hadn't even arrived yet. That's when I thought it best to reserve some joie de vivre for the best yet to come, while unfortunately my mate Dave was getting far too carried away in the bar area and would live to regret it later when the serious stuff started.

Sasha's arrival in the building led to the usual animated murmurings the moment someone caught a glimpse of his slim frame passing through the crowd. A bout of Chinese whispers began to spread the word of his onset. An Elvis-like announcement was never necessary. His distinctive silhouette could be made out with ease against the strategically under-lit background behind the decks. His appearance was greeted with the standard rapturous ovation to which a slight nod of the head would suffice as acknowledgement.

Once headphones were in place around his neck and customary cig lit in hand, it was time for the magic to commence. His typical intro around this time were always trademarked with a variety of noises, bleeps, swirls and echoes that would gradually build into sweeping strings and pianos, announcing his arrival to the stage without the need for any introduction. You just knew.

This 18-month era that ensued after the demise of Shelley's contained some of my fondest memories of clubbing, not only from a music standpoint but in setting the foundations for the future of clubs and the sound of things to come. Anything released by record labels Guerrilla, co-owned by William Orbit, Scotland's Limbo Records and Lisa Horan's Hard Hands imprint that forged the genius of Leftfield were a constant in Sasha's record boxes at the time.

The swirling helicopter sounds and rolling bassline of Disco Evangelists' *De Niro* and the progressive stabs of Havana's *Ethnic Prayer* instantly come to the fore when I conjure up memories of this night. I locked myself into the musical voyage that was unfolding in front of me and that was just from four cans of Budweiser, such was the intensity that Sasha played with.

It was a noticeable move away from the Italian piano anthems he had become so synonymous with, and it marked the start of the so called 'progressive house' movement, a label which illustrated the media's necessity to pigeonhole all the genres of music that were evolving around this time. Saying that, I was quite happy to go along with tags like these, but trying to explain the subtle differences to a colleague at work come Monday morning was like asking me to give you my Renaissance Vol.1 CD. You're just wasting your time. They'd ask in disbelief: "You went where for a night out? London? Are you mad?"

The thought of travelling further than you'd go for a fiver in a taxi from the comforts of home seemed ridiculous, and unbelievably we were just going listening to a DJ play records, not even a live band. The strained expression on colleagues' faces when I tried to explain not only the small matter of this thing called 'house' but that a certain DJ named Sasha was also playing was memorable.

To the football fans around me, I asked them "If Pelé was playing in London on a Friday night, would they consider travelling to see him?" To the female fraternity in the office, I put it to them that it was as if Harrods were giving away free samples of everything in the store for the price of a £10 entrance fee. This was my only way of getting across the message of how big an event this was to house music fraternity. Almost all my colleagues agreed they would have accepted those offers I proposed, though as with life itself it's all about how motivated you are to get yourself off the sofa to go out and enjoy yourself. Yet if you couldn't be arsed at 21, God help you at 31.

As another legendary night with Sasha drew to a close, so did the eyes of my mate Dave, who was literally dead on his feet, wanting to hear the last record more than most just so he could get his head down in the car on the way home.

The names of the last few tunes on this night unfortunately escape me but I do remember the usual packed crowd, hands in the air, baying for more of the same. True to form, they were equally eager to remain rooted to their spots as the lights came up on such a memorable night. There have been times when we have hastily made an early dart for the exit thinking that the last tune had been played

God is a DJ*

and then to our dismay, the magical one would manage to slip another piece of vinyl onto the decks to let the crowd have just one more.

On this occasion, that experience came in useful as the opening bars of another classic track roared through the PA system to the delight of the hardcore who had remained in their hard fought positions. As expected the place went crazy for another few minutes until finally security brought the curtain down at the third time of asking. I think we'd all had our money's worth by this point.

The 5am brightness that greeted us on exiting the club brought about the realisation of where you were and even more surprisingly who you'd been actually standing next to for the last four hours. If you would have asked me how many people were in the main room that night I would probably have said between two and three thousand, such was the apparent enormity of the room and the swarming mass of bodies that filled it

After returning to the Ministry, unbelievably for only the second time, in 2001, I quizzed a friend of mine, Brian Cheetham, who worked and DJed for the Ministry institution, as to whether they had downsized the room that night. It came to light that there would have been probably no more than 800 privileged clubbers there. Then again, I presume all 800 have their own story to tell. The unenviable drive back home to Manchester is another story altogether.

4

Harmony

Haçienda, Manchester, 1992

"Sire, I am from another country. We are bored in the city, there is no longer any Temple of the Sun . . . And you, forgotten . . . without music and without geography, no longer setting out for the hacienda where the roots think of the child and where the wine is finished off with labels from an old almanac. Now that's finished. You'll never see the hacienda. It doesn't exist. The hacienda must be built."

Formulary for a New Urbanism, Ivan Chtcheglov, 1953

"The Haçienda opened my ears to the absolute power of music"

Sasha

IF someone had told me 20 years ago that the Haçienda would be flattened to make way for plush apartments in a new re-urbanisation of the city centre, it would have been the equivalent of someone saying during the same period that a then dominant Liverpool would not be champions of English football again. It would seem unbelievable, such was the dominant force with which the Haçienda loomed over Manchester, much like Liverpool had that grip on the League.

There is often talk of institutions and religions shaping people's lives and the way they live them. Such plaudits could easily be afforded of the Haçienda for many a 20-year-old to early 40-year-old whose weekends from 1987 through to 1994 were governed by the constant evolving of their renowned Friday and Saturday nights respectively.

A derelict former yacht showroom was officially opened as the Haçienda on 21st May 1982 by the late Anthony Wilson and his legendary Factory Records band New Order along with their manager Rob Gretton, initially as a Members Only club. The idea was to try to replicate the venues they had experienced in New York with their very own club.

> I'd been to New York and seen Danceteria and Paradise Garage. I just thought 'Why hasn't Manchester got one of those? Fuckin' New York's got one, we should have one,' stated a resolute Anthony Wilson.

With the pioneering foresight of designers Ben Kelly and Sandra Douglas, the design perfectly echoed the quote from the 1953 essay 'Formulary for a New Urbanism', from which it took its name. They concentrated their vision on the graphic works of artist Peter Saville, who had already worked extensively on album covers and artwork for post-punk band Joy Division and their subsequent guise New Order.

In 1982, when describing this highly accomplished interior, Alistair Best of Architectural Review wrote:

> The steel entrails of the warehouse, tricked out in bright colours, link the old Manchester of hard graft with the new Manchester of superabundant spare time. A significant milestone in British interior design.

For the first five years of its life the venue was virtually empty each night, losing thousands of pounds in the process, mainly due to bad management and promotion with egos and personality clashes a constant detraction to what should have been a booming success story. Only New Order's commercial success during this period prevented the club shutting its doors way before it ever got the chance to be worth remembering.

Mike Pickering was one of the founding DJs who made his name at the club a long time before his self-named band M People came to the fore. His take on the club's formative years was one of mixed feelings.

> We could play whatever we wanted to play. It was Manchester's first 'scally' night, he said. It encompassed all the scenes around at the time, so there were indie type scenes, Perry boys, Motown, Northern Soul. It was a really good night, but it was really Mancunian. I think that had a lot to do with it.

Mike's new Friday night 'Nude' in 1986 turned the club's fortunes around literally overnight with his blend of electro, post-punk disco providing a soundtrack that became the forerunner for the first signs of the house music that grabbed the city's attention by the balls.

This was exactly what the North West of England had been craving since the demise of punk and Northern Soul, and the diverse crowd reflected the eclectic tastes of each individual who soon became part of the furniture. Now the club had been switched on, it was time to turn up the volume.

The year 1988 was dubbed 'The Summer of Love' as Jon DaSilva and Pickering joined forces for their new Wednesday night 'Hot' that lived up to its name in every sense of the word. A swimming pool was added next to the dancefloor and the new drug of the time ecstasy was in the ascendance, young kids paying £15 each for a tablet that would intensify their experience of 'the best night of their lives'.

> *Hot was great for us, Anthony Wilson commented later. Taking Pickering and Park's obscure house music and putting a swimming pool in the club was an excellent idea, so timely. It was at exactly the same moment as the Balearic people dropped the Balearic beats.*

It proved to be another turning point for the Haç with successful nights now being promoted throughout the week. The now legendary queues had now seemingly become permanent from Wednesdays through to Saturdays, snaking round the whole building, six people wide from as early as 8pm, each person with a hope and prayer that they'd be let in for their weekly fix.

During the late Eighties and early Nineties, the city boomed and promoters of various nights around Manchester could be confident of filling a venue on any of the lesser nights of the week. Even Mondays were busy as events such as Ross Mackenzie's 'Most Excellent' at the State flourished thanks to the antics of residents Justin Robertson and Greg Fenton.

Nights like these would go from strength to strength in a short space of time leading to hundreds being locked out each week, such was people's passion to embrace these early house nights. There were no big glossy flyers or adverts in national magazines, just plain and simple word of mouth, with possibly the cooler, more exclusive magazines like *i-D* touting them as nights worth checking in the brief two pages dedicated to clubs.

God is a DJ*

Things have certainly changed. In today's climate it seems only a prime Friday or Saturday night slot will ensure survival. Even the booking of a big name DJ won't guarantee a sell-out anymore. Maybe there has been a subtle cultural change in attitude over the years, or is it the fact that people today are given so much choice? In these seminal years between 1987 and 1992, if one night a week of the music you loved wouldn't suffice, you had to search hard and get there early to quench your thirst for more of the same quality music.

I was always a Friday night man with Mike Pickering's 'Shine', which had evolved out of the first notable DJ partnership between him and Graeme Park, and which built on the reputation left behind by the famous 'Summer of Love' which had established the Haçienda as THE place to go in the country. I liked it so much I bought the T-shirt.

This was a little more underground and serious than Graeme Park's Saturday shenanigans which were more of a US house affair attracting its fair share of females to boot. Shine was full of music heads, wannabe DJs, DJs' girlfriends and people you bumped into on a Wednesday lunchtime at the counter of Eastern Bloc records, each clutching a scrap of paper with a list of tunes from the previous Friday in the hope that they had been finally released.

A while ago, as I wrote this chapter, I had been on my usual pilgrimage to Sankeys Soap, on the opposite side of town to where the Haçienda's remains stand. Thanks to the efforts and foresight of Sacha Lord and Dave Vincent, this filled a rather large void left in my life with regards to being somewhere that good, you went out of necessity rather than an idle possibility.

After the splendid genius of Kerri Chandler had enthralled and captivated me for a good three hours, I exited the club, T-shirt soaked to the skin, hair flattened and feet aching. As we approached our car, a young lad in his late teens/early twenties asked, in a strange accent, the way to the Meridian Hotel. If you haven't had the pleasure of visiting Sankeys yet, be warned that it isn't easy to find and it's even harder to get home from. Instead of giving him a list of directions, we trustingly offered him a lift to his destination. His first excited question on shutting the car door was: "Did any of you ever go to the Haçienda?"

He was South African, over here for the Commonwealth Games, and had been recommended Sankeys by a friend. He listened intently to our ramblings of what was obviously now legend even in parts of

South Africa and continuously interrupted with questions like: "Did you hear Voodoo Ray played in there? Was it as crazy as I've read about? Did you ever hear Sasha play there?"

I can remember going to the Haç probably somewhere in the region of 20 times when Sasha was playing, which I consider quite an achievement as he was only a resident for a short space of time.

From November 1991, the first Wednesday of every month became simply known as 'Sasha Night', and followed regular guest spots at Pickering's legendary 'Shine' on Fridays. These nights were extremely well attended as you would expect, but mainly by those in the know who had been regulars of Shelley's, Shaboo or the Haç. How times change though, as I'm pretty confident not many of you reading this have been clubbing regularly on a Wednesday night recently.

Manchester, being a city steeped in musical tradition, had now fully embraced house music and the Haçienda was the only place to hear it. Any appearance at what is probably one of Sasha's favourite venues of all time was always one to cherish and regale friends with. Those not present on any said night were always left wishing they had been there first hand to enable them to join in the story.

The 'Harmony' night was supposed to be a one-off special dedicated to the memory of Jon of 2 For Joy fame, whose anthems *In A State* and *Let The Bass Kick* had been belted out through the Haçienda PA system on many a night in 1990/91. He had died tragically in a moped accident in Ibiza, though fortunately his girlfriend Emma survived.

The night was to be a celebration of his life and how he loved to live it and he wasn't to be let down. Such was its success that Harmony 2 was organised at the same time the following year. There would be no argument in me saying everyone who went to the first one came back for more of the same the following year.

The first Harmony night I remember was a really muggy summer day for that time of year in the so-called 'Rainy City'. People drove home from work that night with shades on, music blaring and, for those of us fortunate enough to have a convertible, with hoods down.

I had spoken to Sasha that day on the prehistoric British Telecom landline to ask him how much he was looking forward to being back playing in his beloved Haç. His reply was his usual response when I asked him about a gig, his enthusiastic tones tinged with restraint, giving the impression that he was always in control of any given

God is a DJ*

situation yet a little nervous all the same. I, on the other hand, was always eager to get as much information out of him as I could, trying to answer questions for him so that I could ask another one immediately afterwards. This was after all Sasha I was talking to, so I had every excuse to get excited.

Strange as it may seem, this situation hasn't changed much even after 10 years of knowing him. As he has become more and more established and famous, his time has become even more valuable, yet after every conversation I have had with him, there are always another 20 more questions I'd like to ask him, be it about a new record or new recipe.

His almost nervous demeanour, which belies his spectacular impact on house music, never seems to change whether in person or on the phone. His politeness and courteousness always shine through, leaving you with a feeling as if you've just had a great meal at a top restaurant with good company. You come away satisfied.

The Haç was a mere stone's throw away from Sasha's abode, and I had agreed to meet him in there. "Don't forget to put our names on the list," was my parting shot from our earlier conversation. Sasha will probably be the first to admit that he's not the most organised person in the world, recently confessing that his partner in crime, John Digweed, usually plays the role of mum as well as dad when they are touring together. I'm sure I wasn't the first and I certainly won't be the last person he forgets to add to his ever-increasing guest list from time to time. But given his hectic schedule, such oversights can always be easily forgiven though once you're inside, stood on a podium having it!

The usual trio of Gareth, Dave and I had decided to go as well as Gareth's fiancé Nicola, who was to be romantically proposed to on the hallowed ground that was the Haçienda dancefloor at the stroke of midnight on New Year's Eve in 1994.

I was fortunate to be stood next to them at the moment Gareth had popped the question. I couldn't hear any exchange of words due to the booming sound system but I distinctly remember Nicola's shining, welled up eyes looking at me in disbelief as the sound of the remix of Shabba Ranks' *Mr. Loverman* rang round our ears. This track, played by Mike Pickering at the time, also featured heavily in Sasha's sets during his time as resident at Renaissance in Mansfield, which started earlier that year.

Our first port of call on that night out to the Haç would as usual be the Dry Bar on Oldham St, which was also owned by Factory Records but unfortunately was situated miles away from the Haç on the other side of town.

The lack of appropriate pre-club bars would continue to be a problem around this area of Manchester, with the situation ironically only improving after the Haçienda closed down. Today this same district is thriving with at least a dozen quality watering holes, all pandering to the needs of the young clubber and fully equipped with lighting and PA systems and resident DJs. What we would have given for these venues during such a boom period?

Dry had its own identity, like nothing any major city in the UK had seen before, thanks to designer Ben Kelly who had continued his New York theme from the Haçienda with a cool pre-club bar, unlike any pub we had been used to previously. The raw, industrial effect Dry Bar mirrored its big brother the Haç with its wooden floor, clean lines and stainless steel fascias. Instead of a juke box, it boasted real live DJs whose job it was to give you a taste of what you could expect in the Haç.

These features are all now industry standard for such bars but at the start of the Nineties there was nothing to compare it with. It attracted quite a cool crowd and was a favourite for most of the Manchester bands who were prominent at the time such as the Stone Roses, Happy Mondays, Inspiral Carpets and a young, up and coming band called Oasis. Such luminaries made it even more popular for people who wanted to be seen sat next to or drinking in the same venue as their heroes. Hence by 10pm on any given Friday or Saturday night, there was the inevitable queue. On the other hand, gaining entry to Dry was considerably easier than getting into the Haçienda as I'm sure a large contingent can bear testimony. Being knocked back from the Haç at least once in your clubbing career is par for the course. If someone tells you it never happened to them, they were probably a DJ, staff or were lying.

There was a lot of built-up hype and excitement as you pushed into the usual 500 queue, and then there was always the danger of being turned away and sent home with your tail between your legs for not having the right jeans or facial expression.

The guest list side of the queue to the right of the entrance was always a busy commotion of people content to wait for their signal to

God is a DJ*

come forward for a body search with the daunting metal detectors and airport-style walk through. Such measures were introduced following numerous bouts of violence that erupted inside and outside the club in a battle to control the door and its now substantial takings. The problems worsened and culminated in shootings and stabbings becoming a common, almost weekly occurrence.

As ecstasy continued its rise in popularity, the bid to control the supply of drugs increased the competition between rival gangs, leading to the first closure of the club at the beginning of 1991. This lasted for three months, after which the club reassured police that on its reopening, there would be tougher security measures and stringent monitoring of drug use. However, the problem wasn't to go away and the Haçienda became a victim of its own success. This is not to say that the next four or five years would not have some brilliant nights ahead, and people were still leaving having experienced 'the best night of their lives' again for the umpteenth time. And though the violence was always in the background, the queues remained a constant right up until the mid-90s. While the phenomenal Nude on Wednesdays and Dave Haslam's Temperance Club on Thursdays closed due to trouble, they were replaced with almost as successful nights, the crowds at Paul Cons' monthly gay night 'Flesh', and Sasha's Wednesdays proving the point.

Back to that night in 1992, and I fought my way through a smattering of disgruntled punters whose names probably should have been on the list but had obviously been forgotten in the pandemonium as they seemed to repeatedly ask: "Do you know who I am?"

This unfortunate circumstance was to befall us as I proclaimed my name 'plus three' to the man with board and paper in his hand. The hallowed list you would have thought had Microsoft's secret plans for Windows on it; such was the intent with which the person guarded it as he informed us of our absence from it. But as our look of disbelief was sinking in, who would happen to return to the foyer with a supplementary list but the man himself? As I held my position at the head of the queue, not wanting to retreat without some form of protest, Sasha, seeing my forlorn look, acknowledged me with open arms and ushered all four of us past the surly security.

Safe in the knowledge that we were now inside and ready to embark on a majestic night of music and madness, our joy was compounded by the fact that we had also walked in with the man himself. This was the equivalent of being escorted into the playboy mansion by Hugh Heffner.

Your first decision on entering the Haç was always which bar to go to from the choice of three. The main bar at the back of the dancefloor was the biggest, but never usually an option as it was the furthest away. The second one was the Gay Traitor bar to the left of the entrance, accessed via a walk up two flights of stairs, across a balcony and down another flight. Quite a journey, but worth the adventure all the same. It was always good early doors as there was a funky, chilled set being played by the likes of John Macready to an intimate 50 or so revellers, and it was therefore quite busy.

However, that bar was not recommended for late drinking as aside from having to commandeer the numerous steps, it was always too far to get to the toilet if you were feeling under the weather, so to speak. This problem was illustrated to the full one New Year's Eve when it proved one step too far for me as I decorated the second flight with that night's evening meal. Not a pretty sight.

The sneaky third bar was on the same level as the DJ booth, tucked away behind one of the many partitioned walls of cement which added to the industrial ambience that set the Haçienda apart from the other clubs around at that time.

First to the bar as ever, I ordered five cans of the imported Japanese Sapporo beer in all their chrome glory. One such can indeed still stands proudly, full of pens, next to my PC at home as a constant reminder of happy days at the Haç. Four were for me, with the fifth can being for Sasha, which I needed to take to the DJ booth in person. This was far from a hardship as this hallowed room had always been deemed out of bounds to mere mortals. A firm knock on the distinguished black door was required due to the loudness of the monitors in there. Anything less and you could be stood there all night.

I don't remember who opened it but as soon as they did, I didn't need an invitation to enter, such was my eagerness to see what it was really like in the heartbeat of the Haçienda.

Sasha was just about ready to follow Nipper on the decks, with headphones draped around his neck and his first piece of precious vinyl in his hand. He gratefully accepted the shining chrome can of Sapporo, saying: "You're splashing out, aren't ya?" It was probably only 30p a can dearer than your standard Red Stripe, but it was enough ammunition to make a quip about my alleged shallow pockets. Bastard!

Once I had satisfied myself by scanning the interior of the DJ booth and its contents, we shook hands and as the monitor speaker was louder than a Fatboy Slim shirt, I shouted in his ear that I'd see him later. "How cool was that, being inside the hallowed booth with Sasha?" I thought to myself.

I was so hoping that someone had either seen me go in or come out just to bolster my now soaring confidence. To my delight, I was noticed by one of three sisters I had become good friends with, who all frequented the Haç on most weekends and various Sasha gigs. Not sure whether it was Nicola, Marie or Julia who hastily enquired in astonishment: "How did you get in there?"

Anyone who knows me are well aware that I usually get where water can't, I thought, as I strutted downstairs to find my friends in our usual spot, on the steps in front of the dance floor, next to the end alcove from the left. This probably happens in most clubs you frequent, but having a spot in the Haç just held that little bit more esteem.

On a regular Friday night you could usually spot at least a dozen people sharing their habitual position. Familiar faces from Shelley's, Back to Basics and Hacketts littered the dimly lit alcoves of the ground floor directly underneath the DJ booth. You would always be greeted with a nod, a smile or nice peck on the cheek from the usual perspiring faces acknowledging your arrival at your place of residence. It also gave you a sense of belonging, and you almost felt as though should you be missing one week, people would be asking each other of your whereabouts. As if!

The night itself was a blur from the moment I'd found my friends to the last record being played. Quite a few Sapporos had been downed by midnight, leaving me in a very relaxed state, so to speak.

During the height of its popularity, the Haçienda was probably the first club thousands of kids tried ecstasy, but that was never my bag. Two cans of Red Stripe and Sasha's music were enough to send me into a place of ineffable beauty, and his ability to do this has probably never been surpassed by any DJ anywhere. Many would always presume to this day I was having a drug-fuelled night. However this could not be further from the truth.

1 Hidden gem: Those in the know knew where to go – Hackett's, Blackpool, 1990.

2 Living the dream: Delight at Shelley's Laserdome, Longton, 1990.

3 Not to be missed: The year 1991 was an incredible one for Venus, a club that never failed to deliver the best in house music.

6 Grand finale: The last night of the Northern Exposure Tour, Leeds, 1995.

5 Bringing glamour to house: The Corn Exchange was an incredible venue to match the crowd it attracted.

4 Hot date: That one Saturday a month was always worth the two-hour drive – the drive back was rubbish though!

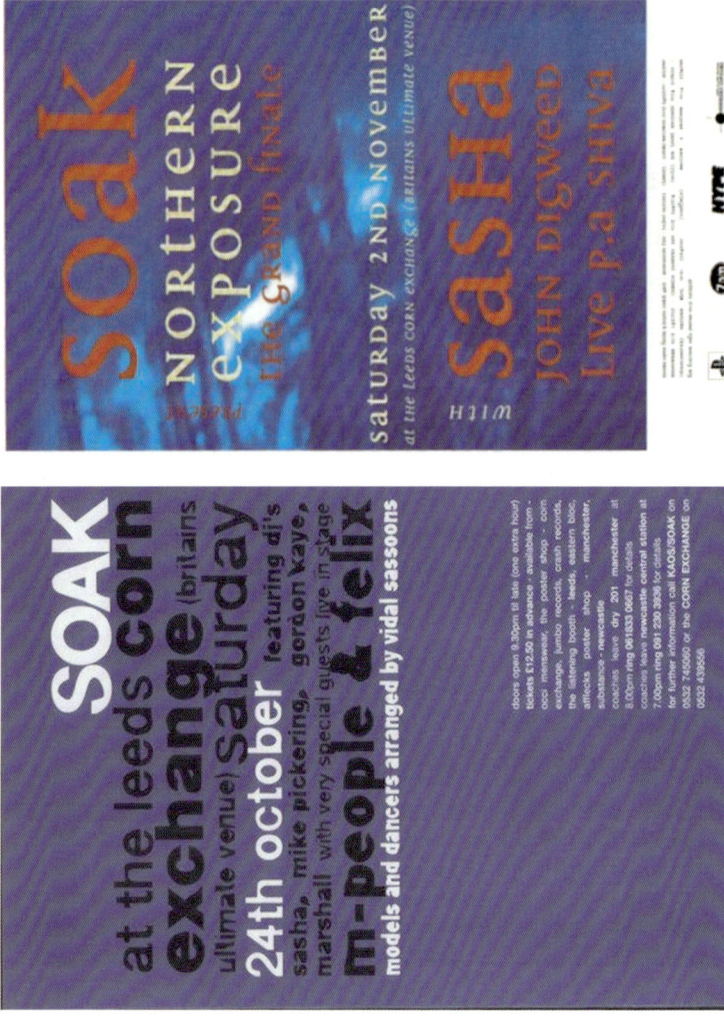

Amazing venue: Shopping in Leeds would never be the same again – The Corn Exchange, 1991.

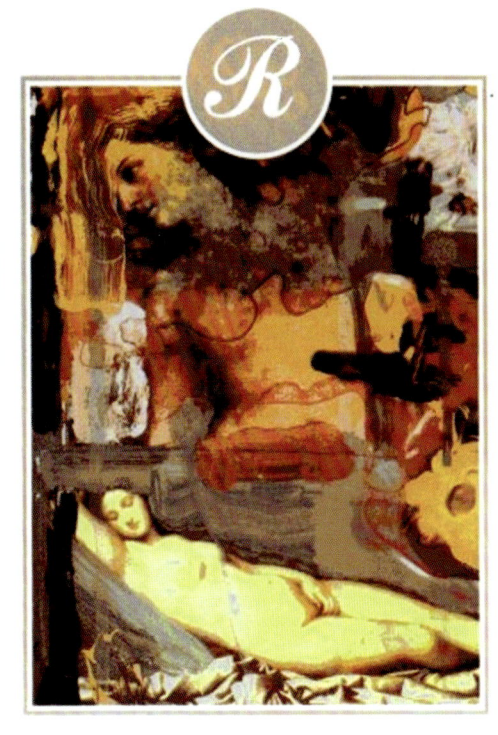

He's back: Sasha's first residency since the closure of Shelley's in 1991 – the original Renaissance at Venue 44, Mansfield.

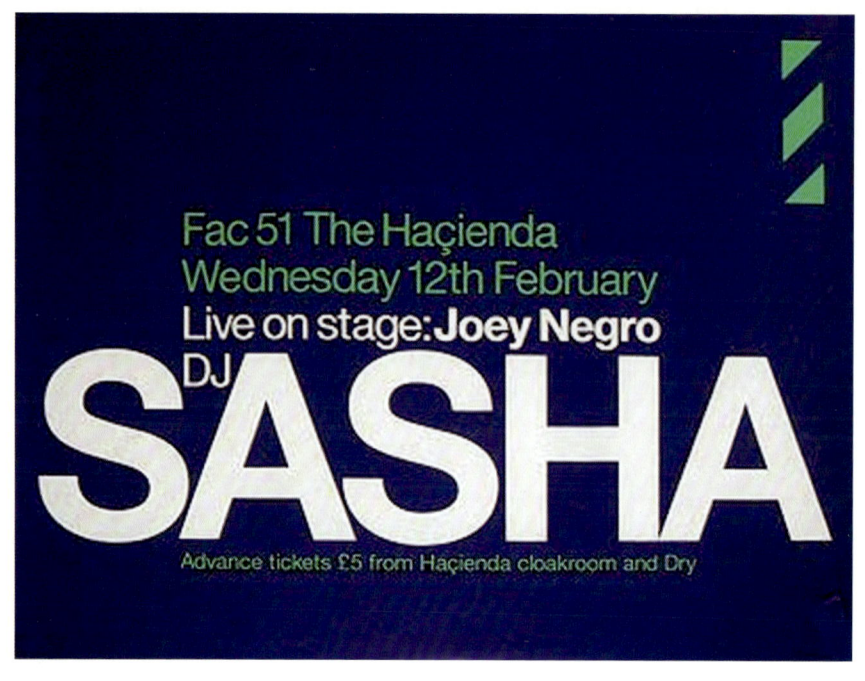

9 Forget the weekend: This was what the middle of the week was all about – The Haçienda, 1992.

10 What Fridays were all about: Shine at The Haçienda, 1992.

Urban icon: The Haçienda, Manchester, 1986–1997 – RIP!

12 Landmark disc: The original mix CD that became the benchmark for what others could only dream of achieving.

15 A step forward: The night Sasha launched the groundbreaking Pioneer CDJ2000.

14 A true 'Summer of Love': It's 1991 and Mixmag brings Sasha to the masses whether he likes it or not.

13 Shape of things to come: But Sasha hated this Mixmag cover from February 1994.

Road trip: The Delta Heavy tour of America with John Digweed, 2002.

17 Sign of the times: A landmark set that confirmed Sasha had gone digital – Circus at The Masque, Liverpool, June 2005.

18 At one with the crowd: Sasha in action, April 2008. (*Courtesy of Jason Warth*)

19 Honorary guest: A landmark night in the history of the Ministry of Sound, September 2009.

20 The cream of Manchester: The Warehouse Project logo.

I always stand by the motto 'each to their own and whatever works for you' but as my friends know, for myself there is no better drug than the music. When that piano break screams through the club's speakers, I always think to myself:

If anyone's feeling better than me at this point, then good luck to them because I'm not far off the ceiling.

One of the most memorable tracks from the night was *Future FJP* by Liaison D whose spring-loaded bassline made this an established favourite with both residents Graeme Park and Mike Pickering. But when Sasha played it, the response was beyond words. The hook line was being hummed by everyone in the place.

Local dance outfit E-lustrious, made up of the guys who had founded Eastern Bloc records, had just released a monster track entitled *Dance No More*. This was already a huge Northern anthem and when the unmistakeable saxophone break, bursting with youthful exuberance, was finally let go, the place went into pandemonium.

The night continued in much the same vein for the last two hours and hit a crescendo on the break of Fast Eddie's anthem *Can U Dance*, with a piano sound that once heard will haunt you forever. It instantly brought a smile to everyone's face and saw arms aloft and air horns and whistles to the fore, making the atmosphere like nowhere else.

Almost every record played that night would be considered a classic by today's standards, making the dancing absolutely relentless. We were extremely reluctant to leave our spot in search of some liquid refreshment as each time you turned to head to the bar, another massive intro familiar with everyone would belt out, leaving you no choice but to join in the madness.

From the stage side of the dancefloor, you could see the silhouette of Sasha with his hand punching the air to the beat, making sure anyone who caught sight of him in full flow responded in similar fashion. Moments like this you can only look back on, aching for the neon-lit signifiers of adolescence with poignant acuity, and congratulate yourselves for being part of history and something that will probably never be repeated.

Sasha's residency was very short-lived and he moved onto pastures new. Along with his departure came that of original DJ Mike Pickering, who finally succumbed to the escalating violence that now littered the

God is a DJ*

club's history after he was held at knifepoint during its 11th birthday celebrations.

This was the final straw not only for Mike but also the police and the club shut its doors for the last time on Saturday, 28th June 1997. Like everything in life, all good things must come to an end, and Sasha had prepared himself for that moment each year he played there.

> *The thing about the days of the Haçienda was we felt like every summer was our last, he said. When it closed the first time in 1991, because of all the trouble, they just put a sign up to say that it was closed and we were all devastated. We thought it was the end of the scene. It would always die off anyway in the winter up north and when it came back in the spring we always felt a relief, like 'Thank God for that!'*

Local lad Elliot Eastwick, who has since DJ'ed around the globe, had the envious task of playing the last ever record at the Haçienda. Unfortunately, he had no idea at the time. A surprise phone call on the Monday following what Elliot thought was another great Saturday night in the history of the Haç told him it was to be the last.

However, not many clubs will get a film made about the history surrounding it, but '24-Hour-Party People' surely must be the icing on a cake which so many can claim to be vital ingredients.

5

Up Yer Ronson/SOAK

Corn Exchange, Leeds, 1992/93

LIKE me and most mere mortals, you probably work in a nine-to-five environment, passing each day looking at the clock too many times.

You may, as I have done, try to sneak a read of your copy of *Muzik*, *Mixmag*, *Ministry* or any listings magazine to choose which night you will fritter your hard earned cash on the coming weekend, even though it's only Monday morning!

It was a rare occurrence indeed, yet one particular weekend I hadn't chosen anything in particular to go to. By the time Friday arrived I had resigned myself to a night at home with Pete Tong, albeit via the 'Essential Selection' on Radio One. Before driving home, I decided to call in at Sasha's house at around 4pm for a cup of tea, talk a bit of music, bollocks and more music and the chance of another precious tape for the car.

I knocked nervously on the door of No.24 even though I had now been here a dozen times, because it was still Sasha's house and I still got excited. His then girlfriend Marie came to the door and warmly welcomed me in with a friendly peck on the cheek and inquired how my week had been.

As I entered the room, Sasha was tied to his decks via his headphones and let on with a nod and his usual nonchalant smile. Sipping a cup of tea, I stood watching Sasha leaning over his decks, inspecting the grooves on his vinyl, looking at the breaks and intros of the latest 50 records that had arrived on his doorstep that week and listening intently to anything that roused interest in his musical psyche.

He would stop intermittently to ask my opinion of a certain sound, and each time I would reply with an enthusiastic approval. Some might have thought I was kissing arse by agreeing with everything he pointed out, but I can honestly say I genuinely loved each section of music replayed to me, never once thinking: "That sounds shit but seeing as you like it I will as well."

God is a DJ*

Meanwhile, I was stood in the kitchen holding court with Marie, inquiring about her shoe designing and how the lads from Evolution, who we both knew from school, were doing. This brief exchange preceded an invite for me to stay for tea. I was not known for passing up on a free feed, and as neither of them had a car I offered to take him to the local Sainsbury's. This was when I first realised that being a top DJ had its advantages over being a top footballer.

On entering the bustling supermarket, I was very conscious of whom I was pushing a trolley for as we perused the fresh herbs section for ingredients from the list Marie had provided. Nobody in the place recognised who he was until we got to the wine section at the farthest aisle away, when a young girl excitedly nudged her friend before whispering to her who exactly was nosing through the New World wine section. Sasha, being Sasha, was completely oblivious to the female attention cast his way, and it is to his credit that this modesty has never waned from his persona.

He readily acknowledged that he is only famous when it goes dark. i.e. behind the confines of club walls, whereas in the cold light of day he is happily left to his own devices in the main to go about his business without the paparazzi following his every move.

It would have probably been around seven o'clock by the time we had finished eating, and as luck would have it Sasha was booked to play 'Up Yer Ronson' at the Music Factory in Leeds that night. The question as to whether to go home and catch the remainder of the 'Essential Selection' or go to Leeds with Sasha and Marie needed two seconds of my attention.

This was one of the biggest Friday nights in the country at the time, run by a good friend of Sasha's, Tony Hannon, who had close links with the equally successful Back to Basics crew who used the same venue on the Saturday night. We wouldn't be travelling alone either as a few more friends were expected at his house at around 9pm to ensure we would be in Leeds for 10pm.

First to arrive was Sasha's closest friend Sparrow, a skinny Brummie lad with a wavy 'curtains' haircut. He had been friends with Sasha from back in the warehouse days during 1988/89 and remained in close contact ever since. Not being the quietest of people, it was hard for Sparrow not to notice me in the open plan house and so we were quickly introduced.

Up Yer Ronson/Soak

A couple more characters arrived, not as colourful as Sparrow but equally charming nonetheless, just in time for the Space Cruiser that was booked to take us to Leeds. Armed with two record boxes, headphones, refreshments and our resident DJ, we were ready to take on Yorkshire and whatever they were prepared to throw at us.

The journey down gave me enough time to acquaint myself with Sparrow. Once I had broken the silence in the car with a tame one liner, he was quick to follow with a joke, much to everyone else's amusement and mine. The following 45-minute journey must have contained a gag a minute as we bounced off each other like Morecambe and Morecambe. I don't want to brag, but Sasha spent his time pissing his sides in the front seat with his neck strained to the rear, unable to get a word in between our double act. You could say we got on from the moment we met.

As we entered Leeds centre, we swept past the Hilton Hotel and took a swift right turn up a one way street, the wrong way. The Music Factory was only a stone's throw away from there and within a minute we had pulled up outside the club. There was a slight queue outside but nothing like the queues that form when Sasha plays Leeds today.

On his recent 'Airdrawndagger' tour to promote his fantastic first solo album of the same name, Sasha took in Dave Beer of Back to Basics' new night Rehab at the old Po Na Na venue not far from where we were heading that night.

Considering it was a Tuesday night, the commotion on both the public and the guest list sides of the queue were equally chaotic with people clambering to get to the right side of the barriers.

Even if your name was down, you still weren't guaranteed entry, which was much to my disgust as I waited outside with a strained neck trying to catch the eye of the diligent Sparrow circulating in the foyer. Much to my dismay I was left on the outside looking in! Even in these days of mobile phones, sometimes it's just too busy to get any kind of response from anyone.

Back to that Friday, and the entrance to the Music Factory, which was basically two substantial black double doors with the venue's title in large white lettering above it, was much understated but it did exactly what it said on the wall.

Promoter Tony Hannon greeted us enthusiastically as we were bang on time. Quite honoured about being 'box boy' yet again, after a quick introduction by Tony I proudly shuffled through the entrance,

God is a DJ*

record box weighing heavy round my knees. Meanwhile the skinny Sparrow, who I reckon got that name on account of his legs, ambled through with ease as though his box's only contents were Sasha's headphones. That's what they call experience.

Sasha had his usual foray of handshakes, hugs and kisses, just from the girls' mind, before he even got through the door.

We were booked to play on the second floor, which was regarded the main floor, and I say 'we' as I carried the boxes, which makes me part of the team. The floor consisted of quite a few intimate alcoves on the right hand side as we entered, while the bar flowed right the way round the room on the left and onto the edge of the main shape-throwing area.

It was a well thought out layout as there would be no queuing at the bar. People who needed to sit down were out of the way and you could easily see the DJ as the booth was in the heart of the dance floor.

I've been to more than a hundred different venues around the country and in most it has been obvious that the DJ booth was an afterthought. It's as though they built the club with no expectation of people dancing or there to be an actual DJ. The Sofa club in Manchester definitely forgot where to put the DJ as he is facing a wall, tucked away in the corner of the dance floor. He is unable to see anyone and his access to the decks is obscured by two large supporting metal columns – but apart from that it's a great venue!

Pacha in Ibiza on the other hand I think built the DJ booth first and then assembled the club around it. As you walk down the opulent stairway leading into the club, the booth looms over the main dance floor perched on a small kind of turret, elevating the DJ so they can survey the crowd with ease. Respect is due to the best club in the world.

Sasha's set during this period was still very much on the vocal side, but he still experimented heavily with the crowd and their reactions, playing Havana's *Ethnic Prayer* and Glam's *Hells Party* alongside Sybil's cover of *The Love I Lost*. Each track was equally well received by the masses that had swarmed onto the main floor, filling any vacant space to get engaged in their full-blown love affair with the dance floor.

A few more cans of Red Stripe and I was locked into the middle of the dance floor, my mind well and truly focused on the mix. It soon started to get sweaty, at which point I wished I had left my leather waistcoat at the door. They were the height of fashion at the time and complemented my black, waxed biker boots and black Diesel jeans, and I thought I looked cool.

I think I'd got into the Cowboy record label more than I'd realised as some young girl decided to adorn me with her glittery cowboy hat. Now I did look the part but it was too late to turn back as I happily waved my finger pistols in the air. I caught sight of Sparrow not far away pissing his sides at my actions. Then again, he wasn't in a much better state as it was only holding onto the bar which stopped him falling over.

The night's crescendo came with the opening bars of none other than Gloria Estefan's *Live for Loving You* which was charting at the time, and was Sasha's number one track of the moment. It's still a beautiful track to this day with nice Latin beats, as you'd expect, warm strings flowing through and a chorus for everyone to join in. I was lucky enough to pick this up as a B-side of one of her ballads released during that period. Not only did I get a free poster with it but it was a mere 95p. Now that's what I call a bargain.

As the chorus kicked in for a second time, the crowd were as one, dancing and prancing, arms in the air and smiles like Cheshire cats. By this stage the cowboy hat had changed heads on numerous occasions but I wasn't prepared to let my waistcoat go with such ease. With hindsight, maybe I should have done just that.

As the last bars of the record beat out to a silence, the hum in my ears started to make itself known, a result of the fact that I had spent the evening in close proximity to one of the main speakers.

The customary handshakes were extended over the decks as the crowd gave Sasha their seal of approval, and chants of 'one more' were hailed at the man like, but he had already played 30 minutes past the 2am curfew and the security were in evacuation mode, bustling people towards the exit and rounding up the stragglers and hangers on as if they were sheep, which seeing as we were in Leeds, I mischievously thought was appropriate. The black bomber jackets formed a dark wall to leave half a dozen of us under the bright lights of a now deserted dance floor, which was swimming in empty cans and bottles.

The magic that had filled the room 15 minutes earlier had now vanished as if attached to the crowd that had just vacated the building. Sasha gathered the spare records that he hadn't had chance to play

God is a DJ*

back into his hallowed box, whilst the rest of us loitered around the booth, some humming the chorus of Miss Estefan's anthem.

A last can of Red Stripe was gratefully received from the promoter but it wasn't as if we needed it, though it would come in handy though for the short journey back over the Pennines.

Once we had loaded everyone onto the Space Cruiser it appeared we had picked up a few new faces, unless I was just seeing double by that stage.

The banter on the journey back had dropped considerably compared to the journey to the club. Everyone appeared to have burnt their respective candles down to the wick in the club, leaving a few nodding heads including Sasha, Marie and Sparrow, then tiredness eventually got the better of me. Before we could contemplate on how the night had evolved, it was 4am and we were back at Fire Station Square, Salford. The stopping of the vehicle was enough to rouse everyone to their senses before we filtered out and into No. 24 to the comfort of central heating and sofas.

Always needing a brew after any kind of exertion, I was first to the kitchen at the rear of the property offering everyone still present and awake a sobering cup of tea or tequila. Sorry to disappoint but tea won hands down and with cup in hands, everyone seemed to vanish to their chosen place of slumber. This left me, a full collection of Laurel and Hardy videos and a strange girl from the night before who hadn't yet acquainted herself. The rest is for me to know ...

Later, using the only form of communication available at the time ie the landline, I phoned my friend Jason to come and pick me up as we had a football match that afternoon at Burnley in the heart of Lancashire, ironically just down the road from where Sasha played one of his first warehouse raves. The team met at the clubhouse at 1pm and if you were late you were fined. A call worth a pound of anyone's money, wouldn't you say?

There were many candidates for the title of having the most prestigious venues outside the capital in the early Nineties, with Manchester and Liverpool staking their claims in the form of the Haçienda and the newly opened Cream respectively, but it was up to Leeds, a city whose nightlife had not yet reached its peak, to defy these beliefs.

The venue chosen to host THE paramount clubbing experience of the year was the Corn Exchange. A lavish glass-domed shopping arcade in the Victorian quarter of Leeds by day, it transformed into a 'clubbers' paradise' by night. The building had become dilapidated since the death of the corn trade at the turn of the century but being one of only two Grade I Listed buildings in Leeds, had undergone a £5million refurbishment to become the focal point of the city centre.

Legendary SOAK/KAOS promoters had held nights at the Warehouse and Pleasure Rooms, both great venues in their own right and always packed to the rafters even on week nights, such was the popularity of these events. They also had a roster of DJs high on the wanted lists of other clubs around the country together with a superb resident in Marshall. They were literally forced to seek out a bigger venue as too many people were leaving disappointed at not being able to gain entry after 10pm due to the crowds that had already swelled each venue to capacity.

The Corn Exchange was not an obvious venue, but nonetheless people who had never been before as either a shopper or a clubber could not fail to be impressed by such an opulent setting with its three tiers, sweeping staircases and overall magnitude.

Fortune favours the brave, as they say, so when Steve Hulme, a 'Mr Fix It' of the rock'n'roll and punk scene in the Seventies and Eighties, managed to blag his way to becoming the official events organiser for the Corn Exchange, he was saddled with the unenviable task of turning such a bespoke venue's fortunes around. The idea of it being turned into some sort of illegal rave at night filled the 40 or so permanent shop owners with dread and so they immediately put in a massive objection to Steve's outrageous proposals. The Fire Department also put their reservations to the fore, limiting the attendance of any event held to less than half its 1,200 capacity, and there were also fears the wooden flooring would collapse.

But then Steve got wind of a fashion show being organised by Vidal Sassoon's regional art director Janet Waddell. Her proposals were to include all the stylish shops in the town centre, including a few in the Corn Exchange, with the event to be held at the popular Warehouse nightclub.

Steve's idea was to get the venue changed and to hold it at the Corn Exchange for a night called 'D-Day', where he would supply the top DJs of the moment including Haçienda favourites Mike Pickering and Jon DaSilva. He went one step further to ensure he had the support of all the shops in the Exchange.

God is a DJ*

We persuaded Yorkshire Television's 'Calendar Fashion Show' to film this unique crossover of fashion and dance music, where the show was just part of the ongoing night's attractions, rather than a focal point at a set time, he explained. This highlighted it so well that we were able to convince the authorities that it was a European type of event and would put Leeds firmly on the map as far as the club scene in this country was concerned. We were granted an occasional entertainment licence for this one-off event which was to be strictly monitored by the authorities. Tickets went on sale at £6.50 and all 1,150 were sold out in advance. There were 75 models on stage showing garments from 30 shops. The DJs on the night were Steve Luigi who played the first set, Jon DaSilva who played a 45 minute set, Mike Pickering who got to play two records at the very end, and Dean White who played throughout the fashion show sets, which took up almost all the night.

The crowd went berserk and the Corn Exchange as a venue was born. Lots of credit must go to Janet Waddell from Vidal Sasoon and Glen Campbell who choreographed the fashion shows. Both believed in the whole concept of a party in a shopping centre.

Fuelled by the success of 'D-Day', London's Flying/Volante records promoter and supremo Charlie Chester was invited to host the subsequent party, again with a fashion show theme courtesy of top designer Michiko Koshino, whose latest range of clothing had become de rigueur in the clubbing world, alongside John Richmond's 'Destroy' label.

This time the show lasted only seven minutes, using a PA from the Tyrell Corporation, with the emphasis now well and truly on the DJs. Flying returned shortly after to host another sold out night and the Corn Exchange was put firmly on the map with local promoters now wanting a piece of the action.

The most frequent habitants were the SOAK/KAOS crew whose weekly nights at The Warehouse, the club that had started the whole commotion, had gained in reputation. The SOAK promoters secured a regular line up of the finest Jocks at the peak of their profiles to entertain and absorb an expectant crowd. The accompanying flyer for the night read not like a 'who's who' but 'who's the bollocks' at that moment in time.

Alongside local boy resident Marshall, who had crafted his own Yorkshire following through various nights and guises around the Leeds area, was Mr M People himself, Mike Pickering. Aside from his pop exploits, he of course had his own massive weekly Friday night, 'Shine' at the Haçienda, though due to his frequent attendance at the 'SOAK' nights, regulars considered him also a resident. Both Marshall and Pickering would play for the first part of the night but the prime two hour slot had been reserved of course for the 'man like' to submerge his audience in aural pleasure.

My entry to the venue was in safe hands as I had arranged to meet Sasha at the entrance around 11pm. Time not being a forte of Sasha's, I stood near the barriers to the entrance, which were now struggling to hold their position due to the multitude of fervent revellers clambering to gain entry to the venue and awaiting his imminent arrival.

After 45 minutes of people surveillance and checking people's dress code, I had perused the guest list queue in its entirety. As anxious as I was to gain entry, the sight of a smattering of industry logo T-shirts made me curious to see if there were any other DJs, known faces or just plain old famous celebrities. Listening to excited banter, I'd established the feel of this well dressed crowd on both sides of the barriers in their Destroy denim, Deakins footwear and serious three-quarter length coats were of sound clubbing background. I was confident another night to remember would ensue.

As the 85th black cab pulled up in front of the swelling crowd outside, the unassuming lone figure of Sasha emerged from the cab door. Laden with two industrial record boxes, he handed me one of the cumbersome boxes to carry. This small gesture of handing over a crate of his magic, probably more valuable than my car come to think of it, gave me a little edge.

As we attempted to make our way into the venue through the heaving masses and heavy security, we were stopped for a search, much to the surprise of everyone in the immediate vicinity, apart from this 'little big man' armed with the almightily powerful black bomber jacket. Thankfully the promoter stepped in to save his blushes as he ushered us through the 20-strong security team, which looked like the New Zealand All Blacks on tour.

We made our passage onto the first floor of this ornate building and towards one of the all-encompassing staircases. The masses

God is a DJ*

parted like a scene from Moses as we made our way up to the third tier. The patting of backs and shaking of hands made the journey to our destination all the more pleasurable, and by this time I had acquired that feeling of celebrity status as people acknowledged the arrival of Sasha and also, I presumed, myself.

On reaching the uppermost level, we were greeted gratefully with yet more handshakes and cold Red Stripe. "Nice touch," I thought, seeing as I wasn't the one driving back to Manchester, and also as I always find beer tastes that bit better when it's free. As Sasha got acquainted with the other dignitaries and DJs, I was left to my own devices to mingle and interact with all and sundry in the best way I knew how. Pretend you know everyone and it puts him or her on the back foot as they think: "Shit. He knows me, I must know him." Works a treat every time.

The last time I had been on the upper tier, apart from a Saturday afternoon shopping, was at another brilliant night run by the same promotions team under the name 'L'America'. Tony Humphries and Todd Terry from the US were headlining the event and were allegedly the highest paid DJs that were playing in the UK at that time, with matching profiles to boot. Humphries, one of the most well respected DJs in the world and a bit of a legend to say the least, acknowledged my presence that night with a slight nod of his head as we stood side by side, leaning over the far-reaching balcony and watching the crowd.

I detected my friends near the bar as usual, in the basement area, drinking their favoured cans of Red Stripe. Then on surveying the remainder of the crowd below, I made eye contact with a familiar attractive female face that always seemed to be in the same club as me, no matter where I was in the country. Looking up in awe, she mouthed through the thumping music: "How did you get up there?" "I'm the DJ", replied Mr Humphries in a similar fashion. "I think she's talking to me," I explained with slight embarrassment. In the words of David Bowie, 'we could be heroes, just for one day'.

Although we were in Leeds, Yorkshire, you could be forgiven for thinking you were somewhere far away from the industrial landscapes of the neighbourhood. As the night progressed, the huge dome warmed to a Balearic temperature reminiscent of a night at El Devino in Ibiza in the height of the season, such was the ambience of the venue.

All three floors, from the basement bar to the top tier, were now brimming with smiling faces, each with a sheen of perspiration giving them that healthy glow. Anyone wearing grey was now regretting this decision due to the large wet patches appearing from armpit to arsehole. Or was that just me being too fashion conscious again?

Fact is I wasn't arsed as the music was just getting better by the DJ. Marshall had warmed the crowd up nicely with a proper house set of four-on-the-floor beats and progressive rumblings that led smoothly into Mike Pickering's introduction. This peaked with the US remix of his own *One Night in Heaven* track, which many were hearing for the first time but which is now firmly cemented as part of UK pop history.

As Sasha took over from the Haçienda marvel to the usual roar of approval for both parties, hands were raised in unison as people waited to hear the first tinkling of his opening record. My memory escapes me on this occasion as to its name but it didn't disappoint nonetheless, with its warm strings floating over some heavy keyboard stabs.

The swirling intro of the track meant the urge to be amongst friends and revellers were proving too much. I descended from the heady heights of the third tier to the first floor where most of action was unfolding. Unfortunately, the waves of people didn't part the same as they did on my entrance, much to my annoyance. My magic celebrity dust had now worn off. In spite of this, after five minutes excusing and squeezing past all and sundry, I was now reacquainted with my mates who had established a position in a cosy little corner aside from the podium at the hub of the dancefloor, almost within touching distance of the 15 foot speakers. This ensured we were close enough to feel the sound reverb through our whole bodies.

With hindsight this position is not recommended for sustained periods on account of the incessant ringing of the ears that proceeds for the entire journey home. At the time though, I was just like a snake being charmed and couldn't help but get drawn nearer and nearer to the thumping black boxes.

Sasha's set teased and tantalised the crowd, with little whispers and stabs of tracks known only by a minority sending a frenzied few into states of delirium, as was his wont. As his set reached its peak, there was a surprise element involving the standout track of the night for me, Within a Dream's *Where is the Feeling*. I had waited anxiously to see whether or not he would play it, having been privileged to an airing of it back at Sasha HQ, Fire Station Square, Manchester. The vivid memory of the big piano break in the song was impregnated on my mind as I had acquired a copy from Eastern Bloc record shop the week before and played it to death from that moment on.

Unfortunately as the track reached its crescendo and with the crowd now at Sasha's mercy, the PA system on the first floor decided to cut out on the exact moment of the piano break. Never has a track so big sounded so little. Or was it just my hearing? The speakers that had pounded my body for the last two to three hours with sonorous beats were now deadly silent. This lasted for what seemed like a whole record but was probably only seconds. I was gutted to say the least.

As the crowd stood stupefied by the momentary silence, the privileged few on the top tier, along with Sasha, where completely oblivious to what had happened. All the monitors above our level had remained at full volume, ensuring all sorts of pandemonium broke out on the balcony where I had previously stood. Then as the PA system kicked back in, the ordinary punters' love affair with the dance floor was soon restored to its full glory and any memory of any temporary break in sound erased from all memories, except mine.

This incident only added to what was another memorable night for many reasons. On vacating the shopping arcade-cum-club, with obligatory damp shirt and flattened hair, the raptures with which people talked excitedly to each other about their favourite part of the night compounded my thoughts that I wouldn't be the only one to remember this event.

As we squeezed through the large double doors, both pushed flush to the wall to enable the masses to filter out, the night air enveloped our bodies and you began hoping your sodden shirt would levitate around your shoulders to stop the icy cotton touching your warm body. Meanwhile, the hub of noise in the street from taxis, cars and clubbers alike was muffled due to dense ringing in my ears. Those bloody enchanting speakers eh?

6

Venus/Renaissance

Nottingham/Mansfield, 1993

FOLLOWING the demise of Shelley's in the early part of 1991, Sasha's future residency was the talk of clubland, with people supposedly in the know inferring that a future weekly night at a secret location in London was on the cards.

It reminded me of pre-season football speculation when the Sunday papers link a top player with four different clubs, only this time it was *Mixmag* and DJ that were responsible for the buzz circulating at the time. I remember feeling cheated that the South were about to take away the best thing that had happened to clubs in the North since I had started to frequent such venues back in 1988.

If there was to be any truth in these rumours, I imagined being left with fleeting guest visits at the Haçienda and other major players in the North at the time. Our alternative would be to travel to London once a month for our Sasha fix, though if this happened I was confident I wouldn't be travelling alone.

To my huge relief, all the speculation was quashed when a sophisticated, expensive looking new flyer handed to me outside the Haç after one particular heady night announced 'the restoration of Sasha to the North'. It had a nice finish to it unlike your standard flyer and even more importantly it was bearing Sasha's name. Everyone who was handed them stopped on the pavement outside the club to take in what they had just read.

Renaissance was the new name on everyone's lips and it was the brainchild of Geoff Oakes. He had become a good friend of Gary McClarnan and Sasha during his time spent at Shelley's. He attended that venue every Friday without fail and the success of the night had obviously rubbed off on Geoff.

He came up with a vision of a new way of clubbing, revealing Renaissance as much more than just a club. It was to become a worldwide brand and a way of life for all who entered its establishment, and who better to cement its reputation than the 'man

God is a DJ*

like?' This was exactly what everyone was waiting for and it was to be Sasha's first residency since that short lived one at his second home, the Haçienda.

Oakes had scrutinised other clubs up and down the country, making mental notes of any bad points and ensuring that he took with him all that was good to put into his new venture. The chosen site for the audacious project was Venue 44 in Mansfield, Nottinghamshire. It received rave reviews from the moment it opened. That was not just because Sasha was the official resident but because the whole set up was pioneering the way forward for the future of clubs. Alongside Cream and the Ministry of Sound, it was to become the third major venue in Britain proclaimed as a 'superclub'.

This was due to the driving force behind the Renaissance concept, promoter Oakes and his team. A focus on attention to detail together with a very selective music policy ensured it wasn't just another club, but a place that unlike no other would take music forward and represent Renaissance in the right way.

Being situated in Mansfield was hardly round the corner for the newly crowned 'Son of God' who didn't have a driving licence and probably never will have, but then would you let it bother you if your main method of transport is the bird in the sky?

As Sasha was still situated in sunny Salford, a weekly return taxi to Nottingham would have proved an inconvenient and expensive commodity, not that money was an issue. It was left to a privileged few of his friends to get him to the venue each week, and I was fortunate enough to be one of those few.

I took the role on a certain Saturday in June, when Sasha was also booked to play one of his and my favourite clubs, Venus in the nearby city of Nottingham, on the same night. This was an awesome venue split between two floors which regularly hosted parties by London's Boys Own, Flying Records and Manchester's own Most Excellent, all of which were highly influential in club culture in these seminal years for house music in Britain.

After loading his record boxes in the boot, Sasha chose to sit in the back seat along with Marie and Gareth. As if taking him to a gig wasn't enough, we were treated to a brand new tape made by his own fair hands earlier that day. This was a ritual he would usually perform to enable him to familiarise himself with a few new tracks that he hadn't had the chance to listen to enough times to ensure he knew the intro/outro of each record.

At the time, one of these tapes was so sought after kids were offering a set of golf clubs in exchange for a copy. Needless to say, this said tape would fortunately never leave my car for the following two months and remains in my possession to this day. The tape opened with Sacha's own collaboration with vocalist Danny Campbell, entitled *Together*, which I had not heard before but remember being immediately hooked on after the first few bars. It had that inimitable Sasha sound to it, with uplifting vocals over layers of emotion.

There was a bit of small talk between us during the next 90 minutes, but we were mostly listening intently to these awesome tracks on the tape, some of which had never been played out yet. I remember feeling very honoured to be not only sat in the same car as someone who was THE DJ in the country in my eyes, but also who was playing his tracks to me and my mates, asking what we thought of a certain track and if we liked the intro to another.

This interest in our opinion just confirmed my thoughts of how important to him it was that we liked and understood the direction he was going in. The style he was to become synonymous with while at Renaissance had taken an all new direction from his legendary screaming sets at Shelley's.

Jokes and banter only really started to flow once we had gone past Leeds and picked up the M1 with signs for Nottingham starting to appear at regular intervals. As the tape clicked off the second side, he waited for our reaction which was of course nothing short of hero worship, but I always find that he is usually genuinely surprised by such praise and always seems to need a kind of reassurance that he is actually quite good.

This tape was followed by 'The Beloved Remixed', which gave myself, Gareth and Dave the chance to bombard the hapless DJ and then girlfriend Marie with question after question from the car. What time did you get up? What's in your box? What did you have for your tea? Really deep, soul-searching stuff like that.

I've always been very conscious of exactly how many questions I actually ask him during a conversation. I have become very aware of how precious his time is and so I end up trying to answer them for him to enable me to get more questions in. But stuck in a car, travelling

God is a DJ*

more than 150 miles to a club, I could relax, as there was nowhere to run.

We were bang on time as we entered the centre of Nottingham. It was bustling by 10pm as people streamed in and out of the various bars and pubs, some making their way home in varying states of drunkenness, others just starting out.

Having been to Venus on a regular basis, we didn't have to suffer the usual driving round the one way system eight times then asking a taxi to guide us to our destination.

As we pulled up outside the club, trying to avoid U-turning taxis dropping off hungry clubbers, our eyes caught the image of a distinctive tartan three-quarter coat filled with the portly figure of James Baillie, promoter of Venus and Sasha's original manager, who was at the packed entrance to greet us.

A considerable queue had already formed down the left-hand side of building. This was usual for a Saturday night but with Sasha in town, the standard two person-wide queues had become probably become seven, leaving the people on the outside spilling into the road. The group of us were shepherded into the club with the minimum of fuss, aside from the mandatory 85 handshakes, pats on the back and kisses. As for Sasha, he had to endure the same.

The main bar area was still as impressive as ever, even to regulars like us, and for those entering for the first time probably more so with its clean, white marble surfaces and pulsating sound system. The bar was situated bang in the middle of the room so you could get served on all four sides, plus it was wide enough to dance on when the night started to really go off, which wasn't far away.

The DJ booth was perched just above head height, just to the side of the entrance, ideally situated to survey the crowd and their reactions. Sasha was booked to play in the main room below, but I knew that on many occasions the atmosphere was so intense in the bar area that many would remain upstairs, not wanting to relinquish their new found private dance floor to soak up the humidity below that nonetheless more than warmed people's emotions.

This night was different from other regular Saturday nights though, as we noticed when Sasha was about to play.

As we made our way down the wide staircase, which was already littered with clubbers well into the swing of things and eager to get a good vantage point for the night ahead, we were followed by what I presumed were the remnants of those in the bar area. The cellar-like room below with a low ceiling and booming sound system had already reached a temperature that made the bar area appear cool in comparison. Danny Rampling was playing to a packed dance floor as we made our way through the crowd and towards the booth in the far corner of the sweltering room. While Sasha prepared himself for his forthcoming set, which would be considered short by today's epic standards, we took our positions in the middle of the dance floor.

We were just in time to catch the end of Danny's eclectic set, which included the Venus anthem *Give You* by D'Jaimin, and Hardfloor's *Acperience*, leaving Sasha with a consummate task of giving the punters more of the same. As he took over the reins from Mr Rampling, the sense of expectancy in the room took an upward turn with the rumbling bars of his opening record.

As usual, from the moment he adorned his headphones his expression noticeably changed from jovial to assiduous. As his head lifted to gauge reaction, he almost looked through people with a stare, taking in the crowd as a whole. The following hour or so passed like a vindaloo on a Sunday morning and before we realised, it was time to pick up our boxes and move swiftly on to our main destination Renaissance, about 11 miles down the road.

Renaissance was one of the first clubs in the country to be granted a late 6am licence and so by the time we arrived at about 2am there were still four hours of clubbing left, much to our delight.

Geoff Oakes, who had spawned the whole idea of making clubbing more than just music in a big room, was on hand at the door to greet us, along with a charming young girl clothed in an outfit straight out of the Spartacus movie. She offered us a selection of fresh fruit from a large silver platter. This was just one of the innovative yet subtle ideas brought to clubland by Oakes to make the night of everyone who entered more pleasurable.

Just like its name, the Mondrian décor to the club matched the corresponding period of Italian culture. All the interior walls were draped in copious amounts of white linen, which covered the usual standard black walls. Hanging from the ceiling were giant cherubs and fluffy white clouds giving the appearance of a manufactured heaven. It was a refreshing and illuminating change to the standard club furnishings. The regulation glitter ball that usually adorns the centre of

God is a DJ*

most club dance floors was replaced with a giant, glittering trademark 'R' which was to become the symbol of Renaissance to this day.

As we entered the main room, probably just after 2am, it had filled up nicely. Some had already decided to make the most of the huge speakers and sub-woofers that were strategically placed in all corners and halfway down the room, by turning them into their very own podiums for the night. The sound was an incredible, immense coalition of noise that surrounded you no matter where you stood.

We started to make our way towards the opposite side of the club when Sasha stopped momentarily and looked up at the DJ booth perched on another level in the furthest corner from where we stood. He instantly recognised the track currently beating out from sound system.

Ian Ossia, a young, up and coming DJ at the time who still remains as one of Renaissance's residents, had been given the task of warming up for the main man, though clearly from the expression on Sasha's face, he was doing the exact opposite. He turned round to me with a look of disbelief.

> I don't fucking believe it, said Sasha. He's playing a track I was going to play at about four o'clock when they really let loose, and he's fucking warming up with it.

Getting to know quite a few DJs in my time and being a vinyl junkie myself a few years back, I have got to know exactly how they work. The minute they hear a record in their respective record shop on Saturday afternoon that blows them away, their very first thought is: "I bet this would sound superb in a club." If they're playing that night, they just can't resist the temptation to play it. But this wasn't just any old bar in the middle of a city centre, playing until last orders for 50 quid. This was Renaissance, THE premier night in the country and there's a certain etiquette to maintain.

But this instant reaction neither perturbed Sasha nor discouraged him. I think it merely made him more determined to administer an even more ferocious set on the mortals below. And boy, were we not disappointed?

The group of us stood for a while at the side of the dancefloor, on the halfway line so to speak, taking in the atmosphere. This was noticeably beginning to build especially as word had filtered through the club that Sasha had arrived and was somewhere in the vicinity of the building, some having already acknowledged his presence with a nod and smile.

It was then time for Sasha to gratefully take the heavy metal box of records that had already lengthened my arms by an inch and make his way through the crowds towards the DJ booth. Gareth, Dave, Marie and I found ourselves a little niche next to one of the main speakers under a massive cardboard cloud suspended above our heads.

The moment Sasha appeared behind the decks, I could've sworn that there was a chink of sunlight behind these artificial clouds that shone in the direction of the elevated booth, as the whole room focused its attention on the main man. At the time he takes to the decks, no matter which club you are in, everyone seems to be waiting for the green light with Sasha acting as the 'traffic light master'.

This particular night's 'amber' record was a track that made the room literally shake. Shabba Ranks' B side of *Mr. Loverman* was like no house record you had ever heard before, but it was a typical Sasha move as only he would have the balls and confidence to know it would not only work but immediately grab people's attention. The shuddering stabs of bass tested the capacity of the PA system to the max and the strength of people's constitution to the full as the ferocious beats pulsed through everyone's body.

This innovative intro was followed by another of his customary epic monsters, full of swirling strings and layers of percussive loops flowing along a river of beats and melodies, and this was just to get your feet wet. Then the opening bars of Mombassa's *Cry Freedom* echoed through the club with its faint African chants simmering over driving tribal beats. This set the mood perfectly for the remainder of the night as he launched into a set that would build and amplify to epic proportions just an hour after it began.

The searing acid breaks and thundering basslines of Age of Love's *Age of Love* sent people into frenzied displays of emotion. This kind of track was perfect for the type of club that Renaissance has become synonymous with, such was the intensity of noise which pushed the PA system to its limits.

The crescendo of the night though came about with the massive, infectious stabs of Felix's *Don't You Want Me?* that went down so well he played it twice, as he did with my favourite track, Brothers Loves Dub's *Mighty Ming*, which was a monster of a record by the irrepressible Dave Seaman under another guise.

God is a DJ*

As Brothers in Rhythm he had made records with particular venues in mind and every time I hear the echoing chants drifting over the tribal beats, it makes me think he had Renaissance in mind when he made it. Both tracks received an even more rapturous response than the first time, podiums filling to the point where some people actually fell off as their hands punched the air with exhilaration.

Such a tumult of devotion towards Sasha continued to pour out for the remainder of the night until 6am when he would reluctantly relinquish his Technics altar only after persistent requests from security to end the night. This was not an exception but a standard offering from a typical Renaissance night that would always end too soon.

Sasha decided to stay on with Marie at one of Geoff Oakes's infamous after-parties, which were known to continue into the early hours of Monday. We had decided to call it a night, only to realise it was actually day as we were blinded by the dazzling sunshine when the exit door opened up to the world of reality and a return journey back to Manchester, which wasn't too bad, unless you were driving.

It's a dirty job but someone's got to do it!

The following decade would see Renaissance move premises not once but three times. The first move was to Conservatory in Derby for three successful years, building a hardcore following of dedicated clubbers educated in the Renaissance way.

This was one venue that unfortunately eluded me in my clubbing exploits, but nevertheless I managed to reintroduce myself to Mr Oakes' establishment following the brave but probably inevitable move to the capital at The Cross. This was a converted railway arch in Charing Cross amongst a glut of other similarly refurbished buildings. It wasn't a plush, eloquent venue replicating the Renaissance style, but nevertheless it suited the style of music played and appealed to a multitude in the capital who were looking for a brand new way of clubbing.

Different in many ways to the original venue in Mansfield, it still held that unmistakable Renaissance feel with its trademark white linen drapes, cherubs and clouds. It still holds a regular monthly slot at this same venue today, a laudable period of time indeed for any clubbing fraternity in today's fickle climate.

Yet even though it has sustained its reputation in the capital, Geoff always hankered to return to his roots in Nottingham where he had started out. Finally he was given the opportunity to do this when after years of refused applications, Nottingham City Council granted him permission to convert a beautiful Grade II listed building right in the centre of Nottingham.

Media, as it was called, was pronounced as the Second Coming of Nottingham clubland and no expense was spared on design. The sweeping staircase that cascaded through the centre of the club was reminiscent of the Guggenheim Museum in New York, while the sound system also took elements from the Big Apple's finest club venues.

Sadly, the Nottingham public did not embrace it for long and it was shamefully turned into a night devoted to the 'School Disco'.

The last time Sasha played at Renaissance was the second birthday party. The following day both he and Geoff would fly to Florida for another gig but unfortunately a massive argument between the two on the plane resulted in them parting and going their separate ways.

Perhaps only the return of the original 'Son of God' would have ensured Renaissance's successful comeback and the 'restoration of Sasha to the North'.

7

Cream and the Big Apple

1995–2002

SOME time during 1995, *Mixmag* proclaimed 'The end of progressive house', and to an extent they were right.

Music had moved on from the early Nineties piano anthems and long epic intros that Sasha and the like had become renowned for, but where it was going now, I for one wasn't sure.

Sasha's residency at Renaissance had ended ironically just after the massive success of his first and in my opinion best compilation CD released to date, *Renaissance Vol. 1*, made in collaboration with partner in crime John Digweed.

My 24th birthday party, held in my flat above my mum's off licence, was a mini-Renaissance party in itself. The three CDs from the compilation were played repeatedly for about eight hours until we had run out of brandy at about six in the morning, by which time everyone knew the playlist like the alphabet.

To celebrate the 10th anniversary of the original mix CD, Renaissance decided to re-release it, and though it is in a re-mastered and re-edited form, nevertheless most of the tracks stood the test of time.

> *It is a very eclectic set, there is a diverse range on the album,* Sasha told Samantha P of the Resident Advisor website. *I guess that's what the word 'progressive' house was about. Somehow, towards the end of the Nineties, it became a genre of its own that didn't really do much and wasn't very exciting to be honest. As soon as that started to happen I started to change, to move away from it. Whenever I go into the studio, I think about making something that is timeless. I want to listen to my records in five or even 10 years' time and the fact that this is being re-released makes me proud. We re-mastered it in the studio. The technology we used back then was so different. There were a couple of tracks that just didn't stand the test of time and as for*

the amounts of pops and clicks we found, I mean how did we not notice them before? We really cleaned it up, gave it a lick of paint, it now sounds remarkably better.

That's more than good enough for me.

Following a spate of panic attacks after a few too many years of excess which culminated in his split with Renaissance, Sasha talked to Rob Fitzpatrick of *Ministry* magazine about getting away from it all to 'get his shit together'.

I did so many drugs at Renaissance, I mean every weekend until I quit, he said. I quit everything and three months later I started getting panic attacks.

Saturday night would end on Tuesday afternoon and because I lived in this little clique in Manchester, it didn't really matter what state I was in. I had no commitments and all I had to get ready for was Renaissance the next weekend.

One night we had some really bad E and I decided to knock it on the head and three months later those panic attacks started. I was watching the U2 Zoo Tour on my TV in my hotel room, getting ready to play the Lakota club in Bristol, and my head just went bang! I locked myself in the bathroom for two hours. I had no idea what was going on or what was going to happen to me? All my senses were heightened and my heart was beating out of my chest. Eventually I was persuaded to come out of the bathroom and go to the gig. As soon as I walked in, the club was just focused on me and everyone was screaming. I felt like I was on acid and tripping. But as soon as I got to the DJ booth and put the needle on the first record, it went.

The following year proved to be one of his biggest battles he had yet to face as he struggled to merely do the job he was being paid for.

I noticed how much the music made it worse, the dark noises in the tunes I was playing triggered these terrible feelings. When I was warming up I was fine but as soon as I started to bang it, I would be flooded with panic. The harder I banged it, the worse I became but the better the crowd reacted. It was a nightmare!

God is a DJ*

A move away from Manchester, to London, unfortunately proved to be a bad choice in trying to find some solace as more vices than ever were on offer. After making a conscious effort to be clean for more than a year, he began to drink heavily which in turn led to spates of insomnia lasting months at a time.

This was a testing time indeed for a young man who had only known the good things for much of his life so far, but coming through it without resorting to the dreaded shrink's couch made him a stronger person.

His attentions turned towards his new partnership with John Digweed, and after a short space of time the pair built up the kind of rapport reserved for brothers and best mates. He was the kind of calming influence Sasha needed in his life. His affiliation with John hadn't had the best of starts. Sasha had been persuaded to go down to what he then considered 'the dreaded South' for John's own night on Hastings Pier in 1990. Sasha was then having the time of his life at Shelley's and couldn't imagine anywhere else being as good.

At the last minute he phoned to cancel, as did some bloke called Paul Oakenfold, leaving John to entertain a rammed club on his own. He managed to pull it off though, with much aplomb, and compounded his reputation as one of the rising 'DJ superstars' as they were soon to become.

It was another three years down the line before he persuaded 'the man like' to play in front of an intimate 200 people on Hastings Pier.

"It was mental. John and I did the last 40 minutes back to back," said Sasha. And the rest, as they say, is history.

This special chemistry went from strength to strength so much so that someone once asked me if Sasha's surname was Digweed, as they never seemed to be discussed in the singular sense anymore.

> *In a way it's quite a strange relationship but we get on really well and speak to each other every week,* John told Mixmag. *No club DJ has ever been such a recognisable figure as Sasha and I think he's done well to handle it. But above all else, he can do the job better than anyone, he really feeds off the crowd.*

Their combined efforts culminated in their second mix compilation, 'Northern Exposure', which was to be a breath of fresh air from the plodding US house that was saturating our clubs back in the UK.

Basically I made my name in the north of England and I never DJed in the South, and John Digweed, even though he is from Hastings on the South Coast, made his name up north, said Sasha. *So when we first started doing gigs in the south of England, we just decided to use this name. I didn't like it. It's kinda cheesy but it just kinda stuck and we then ended up doing that album called 'Northern Exposure'.*

Accompanying the release of this album was a worldwide tour that sealed the return of Sasha after being out of the public eye for a year or so. Following a mini-tour of America, if it's possible to do a mini-tour of the States that is, they cemented relationships with Kimball Collins and Jimmy Van Melleghem in Florida.

Sasha had stayed with the latter before on previous working vacations there, and Jimmy Van M would play a major role in later excursions undertaken by the pair. San Francisco's 'Spundae' night was just one of Sasha's favourite new residencies.

On the other hand, there was a much bigger venue, the city's imposing Civic Hall, for the 'Dance Nation' event that had sold 5,000 tickets. Unfortunately things didn't run as smoothly as first thought and the gig was put off until the following night at a scaled down venue called 10.15.

On their return from America, the duo continued the tour with 18 exclusive gigs throughout the UK including Shindig in Newcastle, the Arches in Glasgow, Brighton's Babelicious, the Haçienda in Manchester of course, and finishing with the Corn Exchange in Leeds.

I caught up with Sasha on the last two gigs that were both well supported. The tour was a roaring success in terms of numbers attending but critically the press, being fickle as they are, didn't warm immediately to the new experiment in sound and beats, struggling to give it a label. They came up with the term 'Epic House' which was to attach itself to the pair for the following couple of years.

Following his split from long-term girlfriend Marie, Sasha had begun to spend more and more time in New York, centring most of his attentions around the club Twilo. The then resident Junior Vasquez had crossed paths with him in 1996 when the club was known as the Sound Factory, during what Sasha describes as his worst ever gig.

He treated me like a complete fucking twat, he told *Mixmag. I'd built myself up to do this gig, so I was over-excited at the*

> prospect. On the night, I was supposed to play for four hours but after an hour these two big guys came in the DJ booth and told me to leave because Junior had arrived. He walked into the booth and wouldn't even catch my eye, let alone say anything to me.
>
> As soon as he started playing these banks of amplifiers, which had been turned off while I was on, suddenly kicked into life. And I wasn't even allowed to leave my records in the booth, I had to take them into the club with me. It was a really humiliating experience.

Despite being a 'twat', and controversially remixing one of Sasha's own tracks *Magic*, Vasquez had helped to craft the awesome Phazon sound system that had been installed in the club. This was the brainchild of engineer Steve Dash who has since changed the sound of so many clubs around the world with his amazing configuration of colossal speakers and woofers. It would rip through the club and anyone who got in its way on any given Saturday for a minimum of around 10 hours until the early hours of the next morning.

While clubs in the UK were still struggling with a 2am licence, New York had a 24 hour policy, something that Sasha could only dream about employing back home. As his reputation travelled across the waters, the one thing Sasha wanted more than anything was to secure a residency at Twilo with partner John Digweed. By April 1998 the dream had become reality.

> They weren't playing our sort of music, so for me and John to go to New York and secure a residency at the most famous nightclub on the planet, where previous DJs were legendary, and create something which was part of the New York night life was really, really special, he said.

Back then in the States, house music was still very much underground, despite the house legends that have emanated from the US, but both were confident of turning this round into a scene similar to that in the UK.

Sasha and John became engrossed in the length of the sets played by the new resident at Twilo, Danny Tenaglia, who would unfold a story that would prey on your emotions. After a tentative start to their residency playing just house, the duo experimented with their sets as the native New Yorkers gradually warmed to the building sound of deep, thundering underground house the pair were championing.

Sasha's description of a typical night at Twilo gives a feel to it.

First up is Jimmy Van M, who plays three hours of wonderful, tripped out E house. He's the perfect DJ to come on after because you can take the music anywhere. The next two hours is all about building it up, playing a lot of that Deep Dish sound. Gradually it gets harder but then you have to watch it, the room can get really excitable, so sometimes you have to hold them back. Otherwise they'll explode and be burnt out by 5am.

Usually by about 4am we'll swap over and then it goes up a gear. Through to 7am it's big records. At 8am we'll take it really hard, not too many breakdowns, just driving European techno which sends everyone loopy. After that we bring it down and we start playing house or breakbeat. The people left at this point are going to be there till the end, so you can pretty much play what you like. Then, for the last hour, we'll bring it back up again.

The first time we played Twilo we thought: 'Right, we're in New York, let's only play house.' It didn't go down too well so we decided to do what we normally do and it really fucking worked.

It wasn't long before queues, reminiscent of scenes back at Shelley's or the Haçienda, began to stretch round the block each time they played. New Year's Day 1998 in New York had reams of kids queuing four or five deep all the way down 10th Avenue, up West 26th and back down West 27th hours before the club opened.

Signs that dance music was well and truly on the move into the mainstream in America and New York in particular were compounded by the release of Sasha and John's 'Communicate' mix compilation in 1998, a very apt title indeed as they had done exactly that with this brand new audience. The album broke into the Top Ten as a new entry, a feat unheard of for dance music artists in the US, and an album signing had been arranged at the biggest Virgin Record Store in the world on Times Square to coincide with the launch. Sasha said:

It's the first DJ mix CD to ever enter into the Billboard 200 and I am very, very proud of that fact.

God is a DJ*

We just really wanted to make a representation of where we're at as DJs at the moment, because there's such confusion between what trance is and what progressive house is. People talk about me in America as a trance DJ, but I consider trance to be the really commercial stuff. I don't like the word at all. So I did this record just to prove to people that you can play intelligent music in the trance genre without cheesing out.

Such was the hysteria surrounding the launch that the police had to block all through roads to cater for the swelling crowds which were reminiscent of personal appearance by the likes of Madonna or Pacino. Sasha described the experience as 'Twilo with the lights on', with both showing signs of embarrassment, particularly when they were asked to play a short set for the demanding crowd. Thankfully the system blew up after three records, much to the relief of the perspiring duo, but to say they had arrived would be an understatement.

Sadly Twilo became the victim of the ruthless Mayor of New York Rudy Giuliani, who closed it down for good due to the discovery of drugs on the premises. Sasha expressed his disappointment to DJ mag.

It was really sad to see Twilo go, he said. We had four amazing years there and made a lot of friends but nothing lasts forever. New York needs a big club like that with that kind of space and sound system.

His reputation in New York at that time was further enhanced when none other than the first lady of music Madonna had declared her interest in him producing a track for her latest album. Arriving back at his hotel in Miami, there was a message saying they wanted Sasha to fly to LA to remix Madonna.

I was jumping around my hotel room, he recalled. However, I actually think by the time I was asked to get involved with the album, she had already finished it. She worked with a French producer and I heard the results were fantastic. I kind of got involved really late so nothing really happened.

I spoke to her a few times and hung out and all. She's really, really cool. Very confident and together. She knows what she wants and she's always on the cutting edge and that's what I respect.

With the help of Brian Transeau, or BT as we know him, he eventually managed not one but two remixes, including the title track *Ray of Light* and *Drowned World/Sky Fits Heaven*.

Back in the UK, in the absence of Sasha and Digweed, I found myself going to nights like Hard Times in Huddersfield listening to the likes of Todd Terry. The venue, an old refurbished church, was a stunning spectacle with its huge, restored leaded glass windows a feature throughout.

The sound system was equally impressive, yet I would just be literally plodding along with the music. It wasn't taking me anywhere or inspiring me any more in the way Sasha had done previously. I began to question the reason why I was going to these places.

I came to the conclusion that if I lose focus on the music then I tend to get distracted by the female of the species. Much as I fought it, I found that in general a larger ratio of girls were going to clubs playing a more US house style and so I followed the crowd and on one night in particular met some brunette girl, whose name escapes me, for a secret rendezvous.

Aside from this highlight, this was the second void in clubland I was experiencing following the closure of the Haçienda. A replacement in venue and style of house music was sought and to my delight the genius of Nick Warren was residing at Cream in Liverpool, which satiated my appetite for new, progressing sounds.

I endeavoured to still catch Sasha whenever he played any one-off nights at venues around the UK and always caught him when he played Cream. He described to Radio 1 the reception he received each time he played as like a homecoming.

Each occasion was always a sell out and the decision on whether he played the 'courtyard' as opposed to the main room would govern whether you would actually get to see him or not, such was the queue to gain access to this legendary back room. The courtyard was always a more intimate affair, later to be inhabited by Paul Oakenfold for two years, and many will regale all and sundry about 'the best night of their lives' there.

I have always been well looked after at Cream since the opening night in October 1992, when Darren Hughes ran it, to the present day

God is a DJ*

under the guise of James Barton and co with the lovely Gill Nightingale always on hand to ensure my entry.

I was fortunate enough to be present for what was to be Sasha's last appearance at Cream in June 2002 when he played to a heaving main room. I say fortunate not only because sadly Cream has now closed its doors but also because of the stunning set he administered onto a crowd willing to absorb all he could throw at them.

This included tracks from his debut *Airdrawndagger* album released later that year, which effortlessly stood up to the test even though they were brand new to most ears. You could see from his smug expression that he was testing the 'up for it' crowds and was more than satisfied with the instant reactions. He had promised something special when I spoke to him in the upstairs bar before he went on and he lived up to his word as usual.

The previous summer, during his last visit to Cream before that final set, I met an old friend called Paul Kane who I had known since frequenting a gem of a night called 'Smile', an underground night that was already thriving well before the opening of Cream in 1992.

With promoter Sam Jones at the helm and resident DJ Paul Myers, who played at that opening night of Cream to about 200 people, there was such a creative force in and around the club at that time. Looking back at the regular faces who attended the Smile night, I am proud to say that I was probably part of one of the most significant underground nights around the North West in the early Nineties.

Almost everyone I encountered in this club has gone on to do their own night, produce their own music or basically be responsible for virtually everything to do with dance music in and around Liverpool. Such faces included the influential James Barton and Darren Hughes as well as Steve Shiels, whose 'Voodoo' night lasted a whole decade. Paul Kane had gone on to form the successful dance duo Desert with Paul Pringle, and when not in the studio or 3 Beat records he had secured himself a residency at Cream from around 1997.

This particular night, Kane was playing early on in the Annexe to quite a significant showing for such an early hour, but then again it was a Sasha night after all and people liked to take their places early on. The Annexe was the original room used when Cream first opened in October 1992. As the club blossomed over the years, it inevitably extended to the larger capacity rooms to cope with demand, leaving the Annexe as the so-called back room.

As Paul finished his set, we stood chatting at the side of the newly refurbished DJ booth along with Gavin from promoters Giant in LA as DJ Darren Emerson stood by while Scouse legend Yousef took the Annexe to another level. The locals went wild and he'd not even put a needle on a record yet.

I noticed Darren was already noticeably consumed with Stella Artois to get him in the mood. The last time I had seen him play was at the Love Parade in Roundhay Park, Leeds to more than 200,000 people. He followed on from Sasha on the main stage. This was timed perfectly as the former Underworld mainstay had collaborated with Sasha on *Scorchio*, a fast, deep, pulsing tech-house track with a cheeky hint of Latin summer carnival. *Scorchio* sums up everything that's best in Sasha's work, deep, intelligent music that still retains a sense of fun and works best out in the middle of the sweaty dancefloor. Hearing *Scorchio* played out for the first time to an incredible reaction from a crowd sent into raptures is one of Sasha's proudest moments.

Ironically, it would be an equally large scale festival where Sasha recalled his worst gig ever.

At Homelands, in England, I probably had the worst set I have ever, ever played in my life. There were 10,000 people in front of me. It was going out live on Radio 1 in England and I had been playing in Mexico City, then flew to New York, then London, and went straight to Homelands.

And they had these decks there which were absolutely horrible as you couldn't even touch the records. You had to use these joysticks to speed the records up and slow them down and I tried two hours of mixing and 10,000 people stood in front of me and ... (shakes head). I went home and I just wanted to slash my wrists.

Just to prove to you that he is human after all.

Back to Cream, and I had promised Paul I'd catch up with him later on in the night, but due to the amount of people passing through the various rooms and lack of signal on my mobile I didn't manage to find him. I spent the remainder of the night trying to access the courtyard where Sasha was playing.

Even adorned with a VIP wristband, I was struggling as access to 'Sasha's room' was restricted to a one in, one out basis such was, and is, his popularity here in the North. Instead Warby and myself stuck it out with Darren Emerson in the Annexe and although his choice of tunes were up to standard, his 'Stella Artois' mixing was something of a let-down.

We fortunately managed to access the courtyard just in time to catch Sasha's protégé James Zabiela's last few CDs. One of the rising stars in the DJ world, he has embraced all that is digital. Some purists bemoan the fact that he has ditched vinyl yet they couldn't help but embrace his so called warm-up set that would befit the master that followed him.

Sasha's two-year absence from Cream was more than worth the wait. All four glorious hours were filled with a roller coaster ride of emotions for all those lucky enough to have squeezed in. The atmosphere was more than electric and the sound overwhelmed some who sought sanctuary on the periphery.

After the final record and a five minute encore of chants for more, he managed to please the crowd one last time with his own *Xpander* track that made the room explode into life for a further 10 minutes.

We stuck it out until security forcibly ejected anyone still standing and we left the building chatting to a couple of girls who had caught a bus to Liverpool from Manchester at around 7pm that evening. They had been in the club since it opened its doors at 9pm to ensure their spot in the courtyard. Whilst they regaled us with their views about how wonderful Sasha had been that night, my mobile phone rang. It was Paul Kane and it was 4.45 in the morning.

Guess where I am? he said.

Sounds like a party to me? I asked inquisitively.

I'm back at James Barton's flat which is only upstairs from me, and Sasha has just taken to the decks playing a classics set!

After excitedly gaining directions, we headed off towards THE after-party, where Sasha did what Coldplay recently wrote that God did and put a smile on everyone's face.

Before he had secured his residency at Twilo with John, I spoke with him in the early part of 1996 at his secluded new home in sleepy Henley-on-Thames, which was a world away from the Big Smoke. Sasha's very own studio was taking shape in the basement, piece by piece, boasting thousands of flashing lights and more knobs than a Ritzy nightclub.

> *The more lights and knobs on the equipment, the more I have to have it. I'm like a kid in a toffee shop, he said. I used to be obsessed with getting the very latest boxes, and I would buy magazines every month to see what the latest box was. I would buy equipment all the time, thinking that's what I needed to do to make the kind of music I wanted to make. But from working with Charlie May, I learned that you only need to know a couple of boxes inside out, and you're set. Charlie does almost all of his work on a couple of specific boxes. He really knows his way around the Yamaha DX7. Once I got out of that buying cycle, I figured out what my favourite boxes were.*

All Sasha's previous productions, such as his own 'QAT Collection', which many refer to as his first solo album, were produced with the help of his faithful engineer Tom Frederikse, who was at his side constantly guiding Sasha through the trials and tribulations of a recording studio.

> *I had already put out* The Qat Collection, *which was just a bunch of club tracks that I had on the shelf, and I thought I'd just go ahead and work on the follow-up. But it didn't work out like that.*

> *Even after I completed* Xpander, *I still felt that I needed to learn my way around the studio. I wanted to make a record that was truly mine, and to do that, I felt I needed to know how to use the equipment in my studio. But when you spend most of your time travelling as a DJ, you don't have the time you need to learn everything.*

With too many remixes to mention having to be completed in major recording studios, such time consuming projects were proving very costly with hire charges at around £600 a day. The extent of work flooding Sasha's way meant more and more time being spent in a studio, and therefore the necessity for his own premises was becoming ever more imperative.

Having also worked extensively with Brian Transeau, aka BT, and Richard Dekkard over a prolonged period of time, he had gained an

God is a DJ*

insight into this new studio world. Their guiding influence and extensive knowledge would prove invaluable to Sasha on the learning curve to constructing his own productions.

> Brian and Richard gave me the confidence to experiment with new equipment and guide me to what was essential for my own studio. Now, on my own, the majority of my spare time is spent experimenting with this new equipment, working towards my own album eventually. However if I need any advice or help then they're only a phone call away.

Brian Transeau had a massive influence on the sounds I myself was searching for with his seminal albums 'IMA' and 'ESCM'. The first album has an epic 42-minute collaboration with 'the man like', culminating in the classic *Embracing the Sunshine* track. The British press dubbed both albums 'epic house', and the sound gave rise to the multi-million selling worldwide smash *Children* by Robert Miles a few years later.

The adjoining room to Sasha's home studio contained his vinyl collection, which had amassed well over 30,000 tracks spanning the length of one side of the room. Sasha's sister Sian kindly endeavoured to give some semblance of order to his vast collection, though some jobs just prove too big. I think she had almost completed the A's after four weeks of digging.

Together with the sounds crafted from the studio, Sasha had enlisted the talents of harpist and flautist Davey Spillaney of Riverdance fame to enable him to expand his own musical capabilities, which currently stand at a modest level 8 on the piano. He had also procured the vocal charms of Maria Nayler, who toured with Evolution and would go on to have her own solo album as well as guesting for the likes of Robert Miles.

Sasha first heard her talents on the Shelley's classic track *Kites* by London based outfit Ultraviolet. He subsequently chose her as lead vocalist on his single *Be As One* which was to be the first single born out of the new studio after two years' hard slog just reading manuals. The equally enchanting B-side, *Heart of Imagination*, is constantly included in Paul Van Dyk's all-time top ten tracks, and he described it as 'having everything'.

The A-side became a Top 20 hit, but should have been far more successful had the single not been bootlegged a few weeks before its official release.

I was gutted, said Sasha. I never even gave a copy of the DAT to Deconstruction. They didn't have it for two or three months. Only John and a few close friends had copies, then two days after the full mail-out, that happens. If a record has been deleted then fair enough, but not this.

As he has been so busy crafting new sounds and with the frequent remix work being thrown his way, DJing has had to take a back seat, but not totally.

It only takes a phone call for me to be tempted into doing a gig. I prefer to turn up unannounced at most venues. However word somehow gets round within a few hours so there's usually a good reception waiting for me wherever it is in the country, and it's not long before I get the bug to do another.

Aided by a constant supply of the latest imports and promos from friends at Eastern Bloc records in Manchester and 3 Beat in Liverpool, Sasha doesn't struggle to keep his finger on the ever-changing sound of house and is no stranger to experimenting with new and different sounds. He talked excitedly about his first album which he enthused at the time could be completed by the year end. I think we both knew then this was an optimistic conjecture nevertheless it compounded his ambition and drive to deliver his best work to date.

During our chat Sasha mentioned a stunning vocalist by the name of Carolyn Lavelle whom he had met during a visit to Peter Gabriel's Real World studio in Bath. She was impressed with the kind of sound he was producing for other artists in his remix work and expressed an interest in Sasha collaborating on a few tracks for her own new album. Unfortunately due to pressure of work and other long term commitments, this partnership was never brought to fruition but 'never say never', as they say.

On one of his visits to the Bath studios, Sasha had invited long-time friend and collaborator BT to take part in what he called 'one of the most amazing musical experiences in my life'.

God is a DJ*

It took place during Real World's annual recording week where artists from all over the world are invited to Bath to record at the famous studios.

We were in there for a week and were just going to do one track, he explained in an article in Mixer magazine. But there were so many talented musicians around and the vibe down there was incredible. People were walking in, hitting things, strumming things, and slapping their goats. There were mad African people everywhere. We ended up recording five tracks and finishing four.

This secret project unfortunately has never been given a full release although a privileged few have heard the finished results. Are you one of them?

Sasha has been known to turn up unannounced at Brian's house, sit him down and force him to listen immediately to new tracks he has come across, and this brought about his contribution on Brian's latest album 'Movement in Still Life'. They also joined forces under the cheeky guise of '2 Phat Cunts' with a one-sided track called *Ride*.

Working with BT however set me back a bit. I used to watch him work in the studio, and he does everything. He's an amazing engineer and programmer. Working with him was extremely inspiring, yet I felt if I was going to write music, I'd have to do the same thing. But BT has spent his entire life in the studio. He has no social life, and he's been locked in the studio for the past 15 years. There's no way I'd have the time or inclination to learn how every single box in the studio works.

John meanwhile was making his own waves with good friend Nick Muir under the guise of 'Bedrock'. This eventually manifested into the now legendary Bedrock night at Heaven nightclub in the heart of London as well as Brighton where he currently resides. Sasha regularly makes guest appearances at both.

Sasha himself had also caught up with the irrepressible former Venus supremo James Baillie and they combined to resurrect the flagging club scene with a brand new night at an old venue. 'Tyrant' at the Bomb is as intimate and intense as you can get in a nightclub with its low ceiling, lack of air conditioning and three feet of space between Sasha, the decks and the usual heaving crowd. Any night Sasha plays here you can virtually taste the next record being mixed in, such is the fervent atmosphere.

> *I run them with Craig Richards. We did it to get away from the whole mainstream thing going on.*

> *Lots of the gigs these days are selling out. The sets are getting cheesier and cheesier, they knock out six or seven mix CDs a year. It's just all money, money, money. Which is fine, I'm in the business to make money, but I also want to make myself happy. I do that by playing the music I want to play. We only started it a year ago and it has already established a very cool and respected name.*

On one of Sasha's many tours of Asia, he followed on from an unknown Lee Burridge at the spectacular Zouk club in Singapore and was blown away with the two hour set that preceded him. Lee was resident there at the time and didn't take much persuading when Sasha asked him to return to the UK to help champion the Tyrant night.

Together with Craig Richards, they took the night to a new level by bringing it to London. It was firstly staged at the End to run in conjunction with their night at the Bomb, but now the nights have amalgamated and found their spiritual home with a spanking new venue to boot at Fabric, London. The PA system installed here was given priority over contemporary fixtures and fittings and boasts serious bass bins under the main dancefloor that make the fillings in your teeth shudder.

Sasha tries to make the gig whenever time permits, as it's a venue he loves to play at, with its unique sound system and cavernous rooms but retaining the intimate feel that was most apparent at Tyrant's previous venues.

The partnership forged by Lee and Craig has enabled the pair to take the Tyrant moniker to the masses, culminating in the release of their own very creditable compilation albums that really bring home that late night Tyrant feeling.

Sasha and John have in the meantime found the scope to conquer parts of America that had not yet succumbed to their powers. Their Delta Heavy Tour of Spring 2002 set out to push the boundaries of perception and imagination, claimed co-conspirator to the event and old time Florida buddy Jimmy Van M, who had the enviable task of setting the mood for each event.

The choice of records played wasn't the only thing to be taken care of as they had employed an arsenal of trucks to convey their favourite Phazon sound system together with visuals and lights provided by Imaginary Forces. The two combined would provide an unforgettable reinvention of the DJ experience that would result in a devastating show of epic proportions.

Sasha was blown away with the opening sequence to the film 'Se7en' and wanted something equally mesmerising to open each event with. Imaginary Forces, who were the visionaries behind this, were employed to develop the Delta Heavy experience by creating a story and look for their entire identity which would in turn become a concept as strong as the music provided.

The tour opened to a fanfare of adulation at the Miami Winter Music Conference, where records are broken and legends made. The lighting and visuals remained constant throughout the tour and although some records remained a staple at virtually all the dates, Sasha and John playing together continued to create something that you could never describe as scripted.

In an interview with *Lunar* magazine, Sasha summed up perfectly why America has fallen head over heels for the S&D experience.

> *We are mixing it up a bit, I mean there are some huge tracks that are played every night, but we don't stick to a set formula. John and I just play our sound. There is just something that you can't put into words when John and I are playing together and it just completely meshes. Not just playing well on our own, but being on the same wavelength all night long. Some nights don't work perfectly like that, but on this tour there have been a lot of those nights.*

Not wanting to be pigeonholed into any particular category, both still strive to be different.

> *I don't really feel that John and I play trance, Sasha responds. That word has such a bad connotation. I really don't care what people categorise me into. I just do my thing that sometimes fits into that trance sound. I was really inspired by the first DJs I ever*

heard at the Haçienda, but I adapted their influence to my own sound.

And what a sound. John is equally defiant about being pigeonholed into one genre.

That whole thing, it's other people's music, he said. If it's that easy, let's see you get up there and do it and get the same reaction. You could give 10 DJs the same records and they would probably all play them differently. But there may only be a few that play them in a way that makes sense and that's the key. I think if you look at it now, a lot of stuff that we play is our own production. I am making records specifically for when I go out to play then I'm doing re-edits of tracks to make them sound better, to fit to how I want them to sound. I think DJs now are being more creative.

The satisfaction with how well the tour was perceived in the US is conveyed in abundance by both Sasha and John, but, keeping it real so to speak, Sasha summed up his emotions whilst on tour.

We played places in America that we'd never been to before, he said. It was a dream to go out with our own sound system and lights. But it was intense, too. Nine weeks on a tour bus is pretty fucking mental.

John and I have worked together for almost 10 years, so we have a friendship that goes beyond music. We've hardly ever had a fight, but if we'd stayed out on the road for a few more weeks, we probably would have ended up strangling each other. But at the end of the day, people have day jobs and work eight hours at a time. I'm just playing records!

With residencies something of an impracticality for Sasha now, it is more imperative than ever to catch him whenever he's in the country, be it Manchester, Birmingham, Seventh Heaven or Cloud Nine.

The journey I have been on with Sasha so far is like jet-black hair and eyesight. It won't last forever and once it's gone you have to resort to poor imitations. My eyesight is fine by the way, and I'm glad to be keeping my silver locks for the time being.

8

Bedrock First Birthday

Heaven, London, October 1999

LIVING on the outskirts of Manchester as we did, London was always a place we tended to travel to for birthday weekends, to see friends, or to visit girls we'd met on holiday that year.

I first started to go to London in 1990 when Phil Perry's 'Full Circle' night was at its peak. This was probably one of the first successful nights to be held on a Sunday. Starting in late afternoon, it catered for the people who weren't satisfied with just a Saturday night and needed a little something extra from their weekends.

In these seminal years, the overwhelming press that Sasha was receiving from various music publications and word of mouth was always met with a little disbelief in the Big Smoke. Although the South had Rampling, Oakenfold and the Boys Own crew, I don't think they could believe that someone could even compare to their leading players, let alone surpass them.

During the following 10 years though, there was an ever-increasing demand for Sasha to travel south of Watford to ply them with his magic.

I would always jump at the chance to spend any time I could in the capital, even if all we could afford was a room for three at the Regent Palace hotel for £45. The accommodation was of little interest to us though, as the whole day would be spent shopping for clothes and records. Any feelings of tiredness would have to wait until Monday, as we were determined to soak up every hour we had.

Fast forward almost 10 years, and to find myself holed up in a hotel in the capital with 20 or so other lads was as good as work gets, and this came about as I had been selected to play for our Manchester region works football side against a London select outfit. The game was played on a Thursday afternoon, which meant travelling that morning on the coach and returning the following day.

By a stroke of good fortune, it was the first Thursday of the month which meant one thing in London for the serious clubbing fraternity,

Bedrock First Birthday

Bedrock night. Sasha's partner in crime John Digweed hosted this monthly night at Heaven nightclub in King's Cross, and this particular Thursday was the event's first birthday party.

So it was a guaranteed night of consummate clubbing to be thrust upon myself and good friends Crafty and Phil, who were fortunate to be in London at the time. Crafty, a northerner by birth, was living in Clapham at the time and was always on hand to put me up on any given week or weekend that I had chance get down to the capital. Phil on the other hand lived just round the corner from me in Manchester but was down there for a spot of business until Friday, staying in Kensington.

Elsewhere in the metropolis, the other major event occurring on this said Thursday was the prestigious annual *Muzik* magazine awards, held at a secret location.

Sasha had spent the week hunting down a suit befitting of a man who was about to collect the prestigious award of 'Outstanding Contribution to Dance Music'. The people in the industry, whose opinion matters, had bestowed such a distinguished award upon him after 10 years of, well, outstanding contributions.

Finding a suit appropriate for a DJ would, you would think, be an impossible mission. I don't remember any of them being in court so I'm trying to remember the last time I saw one of the 'chosen ones' dressed up in anything apart from combats or jeans, let alone matching trousers and jacket. He managed to pull it off though, with the usual subtle style and panache, in a black Dolce & Gabbana number.

His very proud father was present to see him collect this distinguished award along with John, Sparrow, Marie and a host of other close friends who had seen him rise from shy, geeky student to master of the wheels of steel. As you might expect, his acceptance speech was nothing like the Oscars. No tears or political statements, just a lot of thanks and respect.

As the champagne flowed at the awards ceremony, the two Phils and I enjoyed the delights of Mash & Air's special home brew, near downtown Soho. This establishment mirrored its little sister venue back in Manchester, which in its pomp was as popular as the opening night of Space in Ibiza. This made us feel at ease in the hustle and bustle of London town as we sank a good few rounds to get the show on the road.

God is a DJ*

As the time approached midnight, we decided to head for King's Cross tube station as Heaven nightclub was a mere stride away. Although it wasn't quite the weekend yet, it certainly felt like it as we neared the venue due to the volume of people roving the streets at such a late hour. Surely, I thought, they can't all be going to Bedrock?

But as we turned the corner into the well-lit passageway that housed the entrance to the club, we were confronted with a queue eight people wide and 50 metres long, and that was just the guest list side. After half an hour of patiently waiting to see if our names were on the hallowed list, I finally reached the front to inform the industry standard lovely girl with clipboard of our arrival. The young girl perused the names on the list of Sasha's guests and as it was in alphabetical order, easily found mine near the top.

For some reason on reading my name, people repeat it, question it or laugh at it, but one good thing is they never usually forget it. She instantly recognised not just my name but my face, inquiring whether I was at the opening night. When I replied "no", she insisted it must have been another night in the Smoke when Sasha played, as she had definitely ticked my name off a list before. It's always gratifying to be associated with Sasha, who had not yet arrived from the awards ceremony but thankfully had already phoned his list through with my name auspiciously attached.

We picked our VIP wristbands up from the reception inside and waltzed down the short staircase and through the dimly lit entrance to the club, past the massive 'B' hanging on the wall which signified your arrival at Bedrock.

Heaven is made up of a series of railway arches and has a deceptive 'Tardis-like' quality to it. Once inside, the numbers of cavernous rooms you encounter seem never ending. There are probably only about four, but entering from an alternative doorway with a different record playing and you could be mistaken for thinking you have found a forbidden fifth room.

Each room has its own individuality and characteristics though, from the décor to the metal grilled balconies that overlook the dance floors. Each is littered with misshapen, neon-lit bar areas, some of which have been tucked away in a corner whilst others are the main feature like an island in the centre of the room.

All rooms also play their own sound, each with a slightly different slant to the next, playing twisted breaks, chugging, thumping beats and acid hooks that keep each dance floor ticking over nicely. The decision as to which rooms you favour will no doubt change with each visit, but nevertheless the heavy artillery is always saved for the main room.

After a swift perusal of all the rooms, which took the time we needed to finish a can of Red Stripe, we entered the VIP room which was upstairs, just behind the main room. As it was the first birthday party, it was quite lavishly decorated with various drapes and banners and a bar to match, which was strewn with empty Dom Pérignon bottles even at this early hour.

As I scanned the room for familiar faces, I wasn't disappointed or surprised to find the grinning Sparrow propping up the end of the bar just in case it fell over, along with Sasha's long-time friend Marie, both of whom I had not seen for good few years. Just to the side of them was the whole cast of the film 'Human Traffic', who had arrived from the awards to toast their success at the film winning 'Best Soundtrack'.

After a quick reacquaintance, with Marie more than Sparrow, I introduced my two friends and we quickly resumed our affair with the bartender. We opted for a few samples of the numerous overflowing champagne flutes, which as luck would have it filled the corner of the bar that we were stood. With everyone in a celebratory mood, it wasn't long before a complete stranger would stagger past and top you up, much to our delight.

During a short wander past the bar, I had noticed a few characters sneaking down a white corridor. Inquisitively, I followed them whilst both Phils held our spot at the corner of the bar. The corridor took you left to an entrance which led directly onto a metal-grilled balcony, overlooking the main dancefloor, right next to the DJ booth. The floor was already half full with small contingents of lads and girls enjoying their own little party prior to the main act.

After a brief head nodding session, I realised my flute was empty and so headed back to the green room just in time to see the main players of the evening, Sasha and Diggers, enter the room. No announcement was necessary as everyone turned their heads in unison to acknowledge and congratulate the duo, Sasha on his award and John on his night's first birthday. A good enough reason to celebrate if ever there was one.

Sasha had changed out of his D&G 'whistle' and into his usual attire of combats and T-shirt, armed with his box of records ready for the

God is a DJ*

night ahead. I think I was hug number 35 by the time he had made the short journey from one side of the room to where we were stood, having clambered through handshakes and handbags.

He talked to me excitedly of being so proud to have his father present for such a prestigious award and said he was looking forward to playing to such a charged up crowd. I wished him well and confirmed what time he was playing at before he was whisked off to go and ready himself for the last two hours, back to back with John, a rare treat for the Bedrock massive.

We continued quaffing champers in the upstairs lounge, spotting various dignitaries and rogues from the music business and entertainment industry who had arrived straight from the *Muzik* awards to continue the party into the next day. Some were already showing tell-tale signs of an early start to the night, with spilled drinks occurring at an alarming regularity around certain tables.

We decided to venture back downstairs into the mixer and throw a few shapes in the back room to some seriously twisted breaks and beats courtesy of Bedrock resident Adam Freeland. This room was already packed to the rafters with a large proportion of the bar area being taken up by three gyrating, underdressed girls and couple of lads trying their best to emulate their counterparts with their own special moves. Both parties had obviously struggled to find a spot on the dance floor they were comfortable with while I was comforted by the fact that I was getting served three more beers between the long, lithe legs of one of the said 'gyrators'. A much better view than you'd expect in your average local?

The temperature had also risen due to the volume of bodies crammed in to each room, meaning anything more than a T-shirt or bikini top was uncomfortable, much to the delight of the two Phils and myself as all three of us were suitably attired. The heat emitting from the back room was also a good yardstick for how the main room was faring.

At around 1.45am, having limbered up nicely with the spectral breakbeat antics of the fresh young wannabe Freeland, it was time to let loose on the main arena to enjoy for the remaining two hours the delights of John Digweed and his supposed 'surprise' partner Sasha, although I think this was probably the worst kept secret since Bruce Forsyth's wig.

You could feel the sense of expectancy in the air from the moment you walked through any of the arched entrances that surrounded the room and led you immediately onto what was now a heaving dancefloor. Having jostled and pushed our way to the centre of the floor, we made every effort not to relinquish this prime spot where the acoustics enabled you to feel every beat, experience every chord and move in sync to every bassline.

After the driving first bars of Saints and Sinners', *Pushin' Too Hard* rumbled through your torso, you could feel yourself becoming captivated by what was to follow. Directly in front of us, the elevated DJ booth could be made out through the pulsating lights and smoke.

The eminent silhouettes of Sasha and John could be seen swapping places after two or three records, each looming on the shoulder of the other, trying to better each other's last few records played. It was a hard task indeed, but this well-practised routine, stemming from previous joint residencies at Renaissance and Twilo, was pulled off with aplomb. Each record seamlessly mixed into the next whilst building and layering the sound deployed on the heaving mass below. By the way, they were both jumping around, so you could tell how much pleasure they were getting from playing in such a charged atmosphere.

Following on from the pulsating, dynamic soundscape provided by Bluefish's knee trembling *One*, the highlight of the set for me was the percussive splendour of John's self-penned track *Heaven Scent*, named after the venue, which virtually blew the roof off. When fully unleashed, after minutes of teasing us with the opening bars, the floor became one with hands in air and whistles screaming round my ears. This for me was the G-spot of the night.

Everyone in the room was aching for one more record even though it was now well past the 2am curtain call.

It was left to the man of the moment to end the night on with what has become his signature tune. The legendary *Xpander* track exploded through the cavernous venue with glorious echoing synth stabs familiar to all. Pandemonium ensued for an extended last 10 minutes, confirming the track will always be one of Sasha's outstanding contributions to music.

9

We Love Sundays

Space, Ibiza, September 2000–2002

HOLIDAYS with parents can mentally scar you as a child, whether they be good or bad experiences.

You could have been lucky enough to be taken to the Barrier Reef in Australia as a wide-eyed, inquisitive five-year-old, but if you were like me, you just went to a quaint little village called Saundersfoot near Tenby for five years running.

As a child it didn't really matter to me where it was, I loved it all the same, maybe with the exception of the year I set off the fire extinguisher in the hotel. Thinking it was one of Action Man's machine guns was a mistake any little lad could have made, and the toilet on the first floor landing was the ideal hideout for the next three hours or so while the foam and dust settled.

By 1981, we had left Wales behind and embarked on our first family holiday abroad, which was to Malta. The following year though was my favourite by far. Apart from being the same time the World Cup was being played, we had also booked to stay in Ibiza in the lovely resort of Playa D'en Bossa.

Everything about the place was fantastic but being 11 years old, the highlight of my night was the second game of football at about 7pm, shown on the biggest television I had ever seen in the hotel bar.

However, I had no idea that the moment I went to bed at around 10pm, people were starting to get ready for the highlight of their night, a nightclub directly on the opposite side of the road from our hotel.

According to a few young couples my mum spoke to round the pool during the day, it wasn't anything to write home about. But a hundred yards from this was a huge building used as a conference facility. A few years later, it was to be converted into one of the island's superclubs called Space.

As one of life's born organisers, it's usually left to me to sort out a short break for the few of us still left with the remnants of the clubbing bug. August is the standard favourite month for anyone going away and if you're into your music, which I presume anyone reading this is, then for me you're wasting your time looking anywhere for your week's fix except Ibiza.

Radio 1 has had its 'summer special' week during August for the past six years or so. From all accounts this tends to be a horrendously busy time for Ibiza, partly due to the mass publicity aired by the BBC station in the months leading up to the event. Still, the line-up of DJs booked is always as impressive as ever.

Yet for the last three years I have frequented the 'White Isle' on the first week in September. This started as the perfect excuse for us ageing clubbers to reindulge ourselves in its delights to celebrate my best mate Gareth's 30th Birthday on the 16th.

However, 12 days before this event, 4th September, happened to be Sasha's birthday. He is a year older than Gareth and me, and we missed his own 30th do the year before in 1999. But ever since the opening of Home at Space, he has always managed to celebrate his birthday week on this beautiful island, and we were there this time.

Home at Space was brought about by ex-Cream supremo Darren Hughes, who saw it as a way of expanding his brave new venture of Home in Leicester Square, London. Since the sad departure of the London super-club, due to the capital's authorities hammering down on any licence infringements, it has since evolved into the legendary 'We Love Sundays at Space' sessions, which speak for themselves.

Darren and good friend John Kennedy inquired as to whether Sasha would be interested in helping them promote the night for the whole season. Not surprisingly, Sasha jumped at the chance of being involved with one of his favourite venues. He was booked to play monthly Sundays at what has been described by many as 'the best club in the world'.

To get the ball rolling, the talents of John Digweed together with Steve Lawler, Deep Dish, Danny Tenaglia and Sander Kleinenberg, to name just a few, were also enlisted, and it confirmed what everyone had thought. This would be a guaranteed success whatever the competition it would come up against.

Space was the concept of owner Pepe Rosello and took its name basically because of its sheer size.

Attached to the side of this huge, cavernous club was an outdoor open terrace bar frequented after hours by local DJs and promoters.

God is a DJ*

However, following the explosion of acid house in 1988, it was to transform itself. By 1990, British DJ Alex P had leased the terrace and made his first priority a pair of Technics and sound system to match.

Space quickly established itself as one of the main players on the island and so the necessity to expand the capacity came quickly. But instead of expanding the club, the owners decided to extend the terrace and so keep up with the Jones's, and of course Pasha.

In recent years, as the popularity of Ibiza escalated beyond anyone's dreams, the authorities on the island had to place a noise restriction on all open venues due to the expanding sound systems and elongated opening hours. As a result, roofs had to be placed on all open top clubs such as Amnesia, Privilege, which was formerly Ku, and unfortunately Space.

Although many were sceptical at first, the mesh roof that now adorns the terrace is widely accepted by all who frequent Space as part of the furniture, neither detracting nor eliminating any of the elements it had previously held. You can also still hear the roar of the planes that constantly fly overhead and in some strange way add to whatever track is being played at the time.

Space on Sundays is a 22-hour extravaganza open from early Sunday morning at around 8am, though the terrace shuts at midnight and everyone is ushered inside into the darkness of the main club as opposed to the comparatively incandescent terrace.

The 22-hour policy leaves plenty of scope for Sasha to choose as and when he plays, be it early in the night or early in the morning. Whenever he decides to play though, you can always guarantee it to be full to capacity from an early stage, as with any venue Sasha plays.

Myself and 12 other mates, who all fell into the second age category offered on any formal questionnaire, i.e. 25–34, were there primarily to ensure Gareth's 30th birthday was one that would linger on in the memory.

But it would also to help rekindle any burning clubbing embers still flickering from the early Nineties exploits at the Konspiracy, the Haçienda or the Boardwalk, where most had spent their clubbing apprenticeships. All were leading venues centred around Manchester that held fond memories for the majority of the party, who had decided to venture out to the White Isle for possibly the biggest clubbing week of their lives.

In our mixed party of welders, office workers, sparkies, male models and promoters, there were a few Ibiza virgins who would need guiding through the rocky path of what was always going to be a full on week ahead. Some of us had not known each other very long and only through friends of friends had we all come together. But all were very aware that the first night out would be for Sasha's birthday at Space, as that was all I'd gone on about during the three-hour flight from Manchester.

The holiday had not got off to the best of starts due to a six hour delay, which meant we only arrived at our hotel at around two in the afternoon on the Sunday. Having set out late evening the day before, this interrupted everyone's sleeping patterns somewhat, especially with some copious amount of card playing and Carlsberg in the airport bar.

But sleep would have to wait another day as I for one was determined as ever to make sure I was able to attend Space in a conscious state to meet Sasha. Having sorted the room arrangements pretty quickly, we decided to unpack immediately in the quaint but basic room in one of the many 'gorgeous' two-star hotels dotted around San Antonio.

Everyone had agreed to meet downstairs by the poolside bar to discuss who was still up for going to Space, which is located at Playa D'en Bossa on the other side of the island, ironically right next to the airport where we had just come from.

I phoned Sasha around 5ish to announce my arrival on the island and inquire as to the arrangements for the pending night's activities. We chatted for a few minutes about birthdays, age, hangovers and girlfriends, to which I inquired about his stunning girlfriend Zoië.

I had only met Zoië once before, funnily enough at Space, but this was the one in Leeds one Friday night, when she was with her two equally glamorous friends Charlie and another whose name escapes me. All three were sipping champagne giddily at the side of the decks where Sasha was performing another of his mesmerising sets to a packed house as per the norm. We had been introduced to each other in the small VIP room on Sasha's entrance to the club and she had seemed to warm to my excitable banter.

Space in Leeds was also the first time Warby, my room-mate for the holiday, had seen Sasha play since early 1994 when he had been enthralled by him at the legendary Angels nightclub in Burnley,

God is a DJ*

Lancashire. Sasha informed me that he was staying at the owner Pepe's villa and said along with Zoië and friends, his party included the irrepressible Sparrow, who I had not seen since the Bedrock 1st Birthday party and so I was looking forward to catching up with.

After swiftly throwing cases in our respective rooms, everyone congregated around the pool, each with a customary white plastic chair, as we necked our first of many San Miguels. Each person pondered on whether or not they wanted to head back across the island to Space.

As we reached our third bottle, it became apparent that only the hardcore would be venturing so far away. The majority of the party was quite content to give the 'Sunset Strip' a try, as the nearest some had been to Café Del Mar was a CD in HMV.

This left Gareth, Warby and me to head out to what I was pretty confident was going to be the best night of the holiday. For a number of reasons I was glad the main bulk of the party had decided against going to Space. For one, it would be easier for Sasha to accommodate us onto his already escalating guest list. It was also not guaranteed to be everyone's cup of tea, with a number of the lads preferring the more commercial side of house music. Last but not least, with a small group, it's just a lot less 'mither' when it comes to taxis, drinks, meeting and trying to please everyone.

The three of us caught a taxi at about eight in the evening, which is ridiculously early to be heading out in Ibiza, but when Sasha is on the bill no time is too early.

We arrived at the up market resort of Playa D'en Bossa after a swift half hour journey, reacquainting ourselves with the back roads of this quaint, beautiful island that comes alive once the sun sets. And what a sunset! As we approached our destination, the sun had just disappeared behind the skyline.

Still, I knew there would be plenty more opportunities to catch this wonderful spectacle as this was only our first night on the island and I was far more intent on getting to Space on time to meet Sasha.

As we approached the centre of Playa D'en Bossa, we saw the huge, distinctive 10 foot lettering depicting the word 'SPACE' that adorned the side of the club's exterior wall, with its subtle blue backdrop lighting that highlights each letter. It stands out from the front car park like a pork pie at a Bar Mitzvah amidst the low two-storey buildings in the various guises of white hotels and white bars and restaurants.

Directly underneath the eye-catching lettering, I could see a large contingent of people. As this was at the end of the terrace wall, it became clear that they merely formed the back end of the queue, which was at least eight people wide and about 50 metres long, and it was only 8pm. Instead of approaching the club, the three of us decided to lie low at a bar directly across the road and wait for instructions from Sasha, mirroring some kind of military operation about to take place.

As we slurped on our second jug of sangria, chatting about what we thought and hoped he might play that night, the sounds emitting from the terrace whetted our appetite even more. The vocal charms of Cherie Amore and her summer classic *I Don't Want Nobody* boomed out from the confines of the terrace wall, the crowd being faintly heard on backing vocals, joining in on the chorus.

Minutes later my mobile phone started to vibrate in my pocket. As I answered with an inquisitive expression in my voice, I was mighty relieved that it was Sasha confirming that he was just approaching the club in a people carrier and for us to wait outside on the left of the entrance. The three of us quickly downed the remnants of a third jug of sangria and hastily crossed the car park in front of the club, trying to dodge the cars and taxis that pulled up with alarming regularity.

The guest list side of the queue for Space is notorious for being unorganised, very favourable to all locals and above all very choosy, but conversely, walking in with the man who was responsible for the current hysteria, you would think, would have been a breeze.

Far from it! As the people carrier ground to a halt right at the side of the entrance, the side door slid open to reveal a full house and first to emerge from the tinted windowed vehicle was Sasha himself. Dressed in a short sleeve shirt, trainers and some three-quarter length Maharishi combats, he was empty handed as someone else in the pursuing entourage would be responsible for the record boxes.

Later that summer, he would be found semi-conscious, in a ditch along the roadside of Space, wearing just those very pants, clutching a bottle of Jaegermeister. This happened whilst recording his own Ibiza compilation CD for Global Underground.

It is the kind of thing that befalls anyone on a night out with Global Underground's dynamic Geordie duo James and Andy. The first time I

God is a DJ*

met James was outside Café Mambo when he joined resident DJ Pete Gooding and myself for an early evening glass of wine and to watch the sun go down, as was his regular habit now he owned a villa on the island. How civilised, I thought, but then again how first impressions can deceive you.

Sasha spotted me immediately and shouted. We'd not seen one another for about six months and greeted each other likewise with a firm handshake and big hug. He looked really pleased to see us. I reintroduced him to Gareth, who'd not seen him for about six years, and Warby, who had never been formally introduced before but was made up to be treated with such camaraderie by someone he had only worshipped from afar previously.

As we gathered on the other side of the barriers to the club, the taxi had emptied and Sparrow had already jumped on my back as I was in mid-conversation with Sasha's girlfriend Zoië. To my surprise she had remembered me from Space in Leeds earlier that year. I wasn't surprised really as the moment Sasha saw me he shouted "Foghorn!" This has been his nickname for me since we went to Up Yer Ronson in Leeds back in 1992 and I never shut up all the way there. Apparently I reminded him of the Loony Toons cartoon rooster Foghorn Leghorn.

It was very apt that he remembered me with such fondness as Foghorn in the light of what happened the following year, when he had decided to play the terrace from nine until it closed at midnight as opposed to his usual dark hours inside. I had invited my younger brother Christian and a few other Ibiza virgins, Sean, Phil and Wilky, for our now annual trip in September. They had all heard the previous year's participants regaling them about the 'best club they'd ever been to'.

I had confirmed with Sasha my guest list requirements, but as I strode up to locate the Spanish clipboard monitor, I found that technology had now made him surplus to requirements and he had been replaced with some guy sat with a laptop.

As I reached the front of the queue I was asked to hold off spouting my requirements because the guy's mobile phone rang. He answered with his name then continued in English. The person on the other end of the line declared who he was to a reply of: "Sander Who?" A surprising reply, as it was Sander Kleinenberg, who was regularly playing at the club throughout the season, just extending his guest list, much to the disapproval of this guy.

It was now my turn to ask him to confirm "Brendan Blood plus three". To my dismay he replied: "Sorry, no Brendan Blood. There's a Brendan but it's not Blood." It was the worst scenario possible as there would be no way to phone Sasha at this late hour because he had already taken to the decks.

Plan B was to plead with the guest list guy to let me in provisionally to try and see Sasha in person and confirm whose name he had put me under, if any. After some manic persuasion techniques, he agreed and gave me a laminated pass to enter whilst my brother and friends waited with trepidation outside.

But after pushing past the surly door staff and handing in my pass, I was immediately confronted with a wall of people all as eager as each other to obtain a good vantage point to enjoy their hero at work.

I was solely focused on getting to the elevated DJ booth at the back of the terrace. As I looked over the sea of people towards the booth I caught sight of Sasha, in typical DJ mode, head cocked to one side, one hand on the mixer, the other hand holding the cup of his headphones to his ear.

The DJ booth is positioned between the large bar area and the entrance to the main club and is quite a large elevated wooden construction with its own roof, like a small beach hut. The walls to it are about waist height for the DJ but with an extra glass partition on top, to guard the precious wheels of steel.

I literally fought my way through the crowd, trying to catch his eye with each surge forward as I made towards the booth, but he was far too busy entertaining the horde on what was after all his birthday bash. As I got within 20 feet from my destination, the opening chugging bars to Sunscreem's *Perfect Motion* sent the place into frenzy. Instead of fighting it I decided to enjoy myself for five minutes and throw a few shapes with the other like-minded clubbers.

After this short burst of energy, I spotted an opening right at the front of the booth and decided to go for it. I was now stood directly underneath Sasha but completely out of sight, leaving me with the simple task of scaling the booth wall to get level with the glass.

With plenty sangria inside me this held no fears, so I pulled myself up with relative ease. However Sasha had vanished beneath the decks, digging in his box for the next record. As he rose to his feet, the look of astonishment on his face was a picture to behold. It was a pity I couldn't reach my camera as I was holding onto the glass partition to

God is a DJ*

stop me falling, but it would have been one for the scrapbook. He reached out and shook my hand, and I took quite a pleasure from being acknowledged as someone he knew personally.

"What name did you put me down for on the list?" I inquired.

"Shit, I couldn't remember your surname this morning so I put Brendan Foghorn down. I thought you might have second guessed it," he said, grinning in a way I could only laugh at.

My next task was to make my way back through the heaving throng of clubbers I had just fought past. A spot of stage diving might have been in order and possibly a lot quicker, but unfortunately I was a couple of shots of absinthe short of the madness needed to brave it.

Once I had fought my way back outside the club, I saw the entrance to the door was still mayhem as it was 9.30pm and a whisper had flown round that Sasha was playing the terrace instead of inside, ensuring the pandemonium continued for the next few hours at least.

I gathered my party, who had almost given up on me, and we made our way into the club. I was more anxious to get inside than the first timers who were with me as I had already had a taste of what was to come. I was also looking forward to the reaction of the other three as they would have never have seen such a furore of emotions inside any other club, having missed out on Shelley's and Shaboo.

Their jaws were left gaping at their first insight into this legendary venue which was going mad to every record Sasha plied them with. It's not so often you get to hear him play such an eclectic set nowadays and in such an auspicious venue so you needed to seize every moment. It was his birthday and he was going to enjoy himself so why not join in the fun?

I sent my brother Chris to fight his way to the bar for a few San Miguels while I perused the place for anyone I knew amongst the crowd. I immediately spotted the lovely Zoië at the back of the booth. She gave a friendly wave whilst strutting her stuff and mouthed that she'd see me at the end, i.e. midnight from what I could decipher, when Sasha had finished his set.

I had also spotted the other lads in our party that year who had gained entrance under their own steam and pesetas. They were right in the middle of the mayhem, near the main podium at the heart of the dance floor, which is usually satiated with beautiful people voguing to their hearts content.

Such sights are always aesthetically pleasing on the eye from the perimeter of the main floor, from scantily clad, sun-kissed model types gyrating in time with the beats to blissed out hippies and spaced out kids losing themselves into a hypnotic trance like state of euphoria.

On seeing such sights, we decided to get our drinks and go into the mixer, knowing where you aim to stand and where you end up can be two completely different corners of the terrace, such is the jostling for positions on any given Sasha night.

As Todd Terry's classic Orange Lemon track *Dreams of Santa Anna* had exploded, the following two hours went by in a blur with all manner of spaced out atmospherics and shuddering beats thrust upon a cosmopolitan crowd of 'up for it' punters savouring every record.

The real one to savour this year in particular was Groove Armada's massive dub reggae-tinged *Superstylin*. I had spoken to Tom Findlay, one half of Groove Armada, earlier in the year before he took to the stage at the Academy in Manchester. I naively asked if he would be playing *Superstylin* on this said night and then continued to tell him of the moment on the Space terrace when Sasha played the track. I could not find the words to describe the reaction it got when the first chorus broke. The place simply went fucking mental and when Sasha jumps, everybody jumps, which was the text I sent him the following morning.

This commotion continued for the remainder of his set and before I had chance to check the time, the lights had come on, which meant only a few more records would be played if we were lucky. The music came to a halt with rapturous applause and deafening whistles all around. Cameras flashed like paparazzi, even though they weren't supposed to be allowed into the club.

Suddenly Space owner Pepe appeared to take control of the microphone. He requested everyone wish Sasha a happy birthday, to which he modestly took more plaudits, his head bowed in an unassuming manner as if he wasn't worthy of such adulation. This is something he genuinely believes, as shown by the fact that he will frequently ask for reassurance of his ability when chatting the day after a gig, and it is this modesty that stops him from suffering any pretensions.

As the congratulations subsided, he leaned forward and lightly touched the start button on one of the decks which already had the record cued up. As the opening bars of his very own *Xpander* broke out, everyone in the place went wild and it continued for the full eight

God is a DJ*

minutes of the track. Yet again he had sprinkled his own magic dust throughout the terrace, leaving everyone wanting more.

This was only supposed to be the warm up for real action inside the club where everything turned a little darker and more twisted. The majority would continue the party inside for the remaining six hours, but for some, this had been the performance they had paid their hard earned wages to see and they left satisfied and exhausted.

Pepe described his club as a magical place and the reason DJs fight to play there but added that when Sasha plays a record it seems to be connected through his fingers to the soul of the crowd, and I can't argue with him.

Anyway, back to that first year we had returned to Ibiza in 2000 after such a long absence, and Sasha was scheduled to play inside the club with sidekick John Digweed at the peak time of midnight until 4am. This was my first experience of Space so I was wide-eyed and full of sangria, though forget the bushy tail.

Following our swift reintroductions the full entourage, including Gareth, Warby and myself, made our way up the small flight of steps leading to the terrace. As part of the trailing group, we were being counted in by the brusque security until an unwelcoming arm was thrust across my path. Thankfully Zoië had looked round to check everyone was inside as Sasha became submerged in the adoring crowd. A quick exchange of words and actions between Zoië and the security staff and we were free to join in the party, to our huge relief.

It was around 10pm when we entered and the terrace was already bustling. As Sasha caught up with friends and acquaintances near the DJ booth, we acquainted ourselves with the bar. Sparrow wasn't far from the foray and joined us for a chat about, among other things, how good Ibiza still is and what we thought Sasha would play tonight.

Steve Lawler was given the unenviable task of warming the crowd on the terrace prior to Sasha and John taking over the controls inside, but his set was nothing short of exceptional and set the tone for the night. No disrespect to him, but this was probably the first time I had really acknowledged the ability of Steve even though I had heard him play before at Home in London and Cream during his short spell there. From this moment on I would endeavour to catch his set or night wherever he played in the UK.

His final track was his very own *Rise In* which sent the terrace crowd into frenzy. This made the atmosphere perfect to continue the night inside with Messrs. Sasha and Digweed.

No sooner had the last bars beat out on the terrace than an instant queue formed at the entrance to the rear of the club, which was tucked between the DJ booth and the main terrace bar. Everyone surged to gain access to the back room to attain a prime spot for the remainder of the night, resulting in a lot of jostling and pushing on entry.

As I entered the room I wondered whether the club had taken its name literally, as the only lights visible were neon borders to the bar areas and dancefloor. The rest of club was pitch black. Due to the crush at the entrance some people virtually fell into the club, as it was difficult to see where your next step would take you.

The pitch-blackness was also due in part to the pupils of my eyes altering because of the stark contrast with the terrace and its bright pendant lighting lining the perimeter walls. It was as though you had gone from day to night in an instant. The contrast of lighting was very clever in a subtle way, because as you entered the darkness of the club, the music turned to a more dark, twisted affair, not for the faint hearted.

The tribal beats of Danny Tenaglia's *Datar B* rumbled through the club towards the entrance, where the bass could be felt pulsing from the speakers inside. Starting their set with this track was a sure indication that the night would only get bigger than the monster of a track that had started proceedings.

The sounds of deep house, spaced out breakbeats and twisted trance are layered on top of each other, building the energy in the club. This process, which Sasha mastered in his very early days of DJing, means he has the ability to connect himself through turntables into the dance floor.

As the night gained momentum so did I, so much so that I ended up about 15 feet in the air after scaling the massive podium that shadowed the main floor, directly in front of the DJ booth. From this ideal vantage point, as well as being able to soak up the atmosphere I could scrutinise the working relationship between Sasha and John.

They swapped positions after playing three tracks and the other took over, the duo constantly trying to out-do each other's last mini-

God is a DJ*

set whilst swapping banter in between. It was obvious how much each were enjoying playing to such a receptive room.

The night peaked at around 3am following the massive Bedrock remix of Underworld's *Cowgirl*. As the sun-kissed opening bars of Sasha's own *Scorchio* track wafted over all and sundry, I took out my camera to catch the moment. As he surveyed the room for the reaction he gazed upwards, caught sight of me and pointed my way.

It would have been a great picture but the film, full of great shots from the night, was never developed due to a certain acquaintance of mine called Smithy. I had foolishly given him the finished film to the following night to look after due to my lack of pockets. His subsequent tentative knock on our hotel room door later on was a dead giveaway that he had come bearing bad news.

As he stood near the balcony window and told us of his unfortunate mishap Warby, who was lying on his bed reading Dave Haslam's latest publication *Adventures on the Wheels of Steel*, reacted by throwing the said book at him in disgust. It missed and hit the balcony railing, splitting it in half, leaving the half he had already read on the floor and the other in a tree out on some wasteland out of reach. Some guys have all the luck eh?

Perhaps it was only fitting that for Global Underground's worldwide compilation series, the man chosen for the Ibiza edition is Sasha. After all, who else affiliates himself better with the White Isle?

After so many successful years DJing around the globe, his army of fans, his peers, associates and friends would agree the names Sasha and Space go together like Technics and turntables. So many people can't be wrong.

10

Midweek Session

Club Code, Birmingham, October 2000

THE set up of clubs has been transformed somewhat over the last 20 years since I first started frequenting them.

I'm pleased to say that virtually every aspect has improved, from the sound systems, the toilets and the security down to the cloakrooms. Each piece of the jigsaw that makes a night a success has had attention to detail paid to it.

There is one part of a club in particular that has become more apparent with the explosion of house music in the UK and that's the VIP room.

Back in the early '90s, such rooms did not exist even at some of the larger capacity venues.

However as with anything in life, success brings expansion and demand. DJs gained popularity and some notoriety, largely due to the iconic figures of Sasha, Oakenfold, Sanchez et al that the media elevated to hero status. Along with a couple of boxes of records, many of the American DJs in particular would bring an entourage of friends, managers, girls and hangers on who they expected the promoter of any given night to look after, hence the necessity for a separate room to 'house' them in.

Of all the rooms I have been in though, only a few have made me feel very important, the rest having, as they say, the feeling of a damp squib.

I had accompanied Sasha since his early forays up and down the country, and one Saturday night in the summer of 1994, he had asked me to drive him to Birmingham.

The night he was booked to play was called 'Sacred', and was a spin-off from Geoff Oakes' Renaissance empire. The venue to host this night was the Que Club in the heart of Birmingham city centre, owned by then Duran Duran heartthrob John Taylor.

On arrival, we parked only yards from the entrance. The queue was like the M6, not as wide but just as busy, as people hung onto the

God is a DJ*

edge of the pavement so as not to get sent to the back by the security patrolling the large gathering. This initial sight confirmed the status of Renaissance in the Midlands as the number one night to go to. This was meant to be its little sister, but looked like it would turn out to be its big brother!

The Que Club had a capacity of around 1,600 and was every bit a Renaissance venue in the making as it was after all a Grade II listed building. The grand entrance depicted Birmingham's historical landmarks and its huge sweeping staircase was adorned by a series of specially commissioned murals.

From a quick scan of the queue, I could tell this was very much a VIP night by the dress sense of the crowd, the lads in their best Armani and Paul Smith and many of the girls in slinky summer dresses with suntans to match. The party of five of us breezed past the queue with a few shouts of "Go on Sasha, give it to us!" Fortunately, that was the lads shouting, as had it been a girl, I think then girlfriend Marie would have been a little put out.

Promoter Geoff Oakes wasn't on the door to greet us so instead Sasha relieved me of a box of records and headed off in search of him to confirm our arrival.

We had been greeted by a pretty young blonde girl. Well, they wouldn't hire some extra from Prisoner Cell Block H to greet people would they? She had escorted us from the door and inquired as to whether we would like to go with her into the VIP room.

This was to be my first experience of such rooms. Gareth and Dave, my usual clubbing partners, had made the trip along with Marie, Sasha and myself, and the four of us were taken through a large ornate door that led to a rather steep flight of stairs.

Through the door at the top of the stairs was a large, square room with a bar to the left filling the length of the wall. Deep red velour sofas divided the room into quarters, facing each other in groups of four, whilst to the right of us was a floor to ceiling wall of glass. As I got nearer, I could see that the panes of glass sloped away from me. Having got within touching distance of the glass, I stretched to see what was beneath. The view was spectacular, directly overlooking the dance floor and the second level of the club with its balconies and secluded hideaways.

The VIP room lived up to and exceeded all expectations except for one thing, VIPs! We were the only ones in there, excluding the bar staff. The bass coming from the club was pulsing through the glass and floor leaving us feeling a little left out. Needless to say, we drank a few swift free beers before we hastily made our way down to the main action to find out whether Sasha had started his set and what we were missing out on.

The night only got better from the minute he put his first record on the turntables to the minute we left the club at around 3am.

Unlike us, Sasha had decided to stay on in Birmingham with Marie and a host of other revellers who I presumed would take full advantage of the VIP room, unlike us VIP virgins who had come too early.

Everyone improves with experience and a moment I look back on with mixed feelings is when I went behind the DJ booth to tell Sasha we were heading back to Manchester. This was probably a form of insult to him as he had a good hour left in his set, and his puzzled expression told a story. On reflection, I suppose it was like arriving with Oasis at a gig only to leave before they had played their last tracks, as of course bands and DJs alike save their best till last.

As I was the one driving that night, it was probably my decision to leave early for whatever reason. It was never the fact that the music wasn't right but more than likely my sober frame of mind. I suppose I took it for granted that I could see Sasha play anytime, yet this moment stays with me and I have since been far more aware that his performance really does matter to all those who come to hear and see him play, in particular those closest to him.

It would be almost a decade before I returned to the concrete capital, aside from a fleeting visit via a stag do at Miss Moneypenny's, which frankly didn't hold any fond memories for me to evoke.

Some of the best clubs in the world have evolved in the most unlikely places, from the disused warehouses in New York and Manchester to the underground car parks of Las Vegas to shopping centres in Leeds. But an old bus cleaning depot in Birmingham next to a custard factory was surely stretching the limits of imagination.

Club Code was a purpose built venue born out of this dilapidated depot that was to hopefully resurrect Birmingham's floundering club scene to enable it to compete with the other major cities in the UK.

Godskitchen owner Chris Griffin had been promoting his own successful night at the Sanctuary since 1997, but after a few years the relationship with the club became somewhat strained and he began to

God is a DJ*

shop around for a new venue to continue the night's steady progression. To instigate this he sought guidance and backing form close friend Neil Moffitt who gave Chris and his Godskitchen crew the push they were waiting for to enable them to own their own club outright.

Code was a state of the art venue with a 1,650 capacity, enabling the brand to push new boundaries and expand the way a so-called 'super club' should. It was to rival Liverpool's Cream and London's *Ministry*, though how long it would sustain its pulling power, only time would tell.

The night that would grab my attention was not the much-hyped Saturday night but a far more underground affair hosted by the much lauded Steve Lawler, who had captured my imagination on the Space terrace a year earlier. This period was part of his two year residency there, earning him the fitting title 'King of the Terrace'.

I had followed his career from the time he had returned from Ibiza as Café Mambo resident. It was then Darren Hughes of Cream and now Home@Space recognised his talent and ambition to succeed, signing him up to Cream's DJing agency. That led to Steve beginning a residency at the eponymous Liverpool institution, where at only his second date at the club he had to follow Paul Oakenfold at their NYE party. Not an easy feat, but one which he coped with admirably.

His reputation here gained him the wings to fly down to the Big Smoke with a residency at the glorious yet transient Home in London's Leicester Square. As one door closes another opens, as they say, and it was with great fortune or, as I like to think, destiny, that he was offered the chance of a monthly residency at my beloved local Friday night excursion, Tribal Sessions at Sankeys Soap in Manchester. His regular appearances here together with his own monthly 'Harlem Nights' at the End in London have brought him the reputation as one of the premier DJs in the country and he is currently pushing the tribal sound forward.

Steve has come such a long way from his own self-promoted, illegal tunnel parties underneath the M42 motorway during the early Nineties. The success of these parties, in particular the last one, gave him the confidence to realise that he could make a living doing exactly what he loved to do.

Midweek Session

The last one was just amazing, he said. We had Tony De Vit playing, and it had just grown from this small party to this huge thing, basically a rave. It was all about town the day before, people running around Birmingham going 'The tunnel's on, the tunnel's on.'

And so followed a trip to Ibiza where Steve attained that much privileged residency at Café Mambo with a staple eight hour set as the routine working day. He has since become recognised by his peers as one of the hardest working DJs in the industry.

I had spoken to the ever helpful Clare Woodcock at Global Underground, where Steve had recently launched their Nu Breed mix compilation series, and she had already forewarned me of a new night in the offing. The launch night was to be on a Wednesday and called the 'Midweek Session'. His headline guest booked to play was the one and only Sasha. Steve's style, with his progressive tribal rumblings of drums and haunting chants, always I feel compliments Sasha's darker, more twisted beats.

And so the formula would be set for one of 'THE' nights out of the year and not to be missed for any reason. I phoned Sasha earlier in the week to firstly check his whereabouts. I have found it's always best to phone him at around 6pm so that wherever he is in the world it never too late to phone or too early to wake him.

Luckily he was in Ibiza for his monthly shenanigans, relaxing after another marathon session at Space, and was in good spirits. After a brief chat about the ups and downs of our two opposing lives, I gave him my guest list requirements. I always imagine him lying on a sun lounger by a pool, writing down names on the back of a packet of Marlboro Lights whilst holding the phone between his neck and shoulder. Oh, how the other half live, eh?

As I've said, I have found through previous experience that a new club in a different city from your own is always fraught with missed junctions, wrong turns and bad directions from locals. Aside from this, Birmingham is littered with roundabouts leading many people to believe Spaghetti Junction is a term to describe Birmingham city centre.

Together with fellow promoter Garry Lomas, his brother Paul, who was bequeathed with the title of designated driver for the night, and their cousin Jeff, we left Manchester at 9pm. This left us plenty of time

God is a DJ*

to get lost and find ourselves again. After all it is only 80 miles down the M6 motorway.

To our astonishment we found the venue from the tiny map shown on the back of the flyer I had picked up from Sankeys Soap nightclub the previous week. The huge custard factory signpost was the first landmark we spotted and so we took the first left after this down the side of an original Georgian pub on the corner. Immediately under a railway bridge, a massive block building confronted us with just a door spoiling its perimeter wall. The roof was subtly lit with blue neon light that surrounded its perimeter and the word 'CODE' vertically hung on the first visible corner of the club in huge black and white lettering.

The usual queue had already formed at the entrance even though we were quite early for what was to be an expected late night with a 4am licence confirmed on the flyer.

Being situated in a stark industrial landscape, parking nearby has never been an issue at this venue. We parked under the adjacent archway to the club, which we occupied on each subsequent journey we would make over the next year or so, just like your favourite dancing spot.

The friends I had travelled down with were eager with excitement for a number of reasons. For a start it was a brand new club for all of us and so we were anxious to scrutinise the ins and outs of the much-hyped project, but also the fact that my friends had never been on a guest list before, let alone Sasha's hallowed list, was pretty exciting.

A pretty blonde girl with a nice smile was on hand to greet us at the entrance. I inquired as to whether Sasha had faxed or emailed his list through to the club yet, to which the endearing girl with the clipboard informed me that he'd not sent it in yet. Uncharacteristically for some door staff, she inquired where we had travelled from and how we knew Sasha. To compound what a nice girl she was, she asked if we would like to go in and she'd let Sasha know we were already inside when he eventually arrived.

At this point I decided to phone him to see exactly how far away he was from his destination. He answered in his usual laid back manner as though time was of little importance, but then I presume that is how Sasha stays so calm and collected as opposed to promoters who never relax until the following morning when it's all over.

After Sasha's appearance at the opening night, I only missed two of Steve's 'Midweek Sessions', such was the quality of his guest DJs including head honcho Pete Tong and the legendary Danny Tenaglia. And over the following months, on each visit to the concrete capital we would afford ourselves a few hours before entering the club, trying different bars every time.

Having familiarised myself with the trappings of Birmingham's nightlife that the last Wednesday in the month had to offer, I settled on this night for what remains one of my favourite pre club bars, 52 degrees North. In the heart of the city centre, it provides everything I require from a bar prior to going to a club and the journey from bar to club is minutes in a car, only five roundabouts away. The layout is very opulent, from its cavernous lounge seating to the cool, chic elongated bar, with service to match.

A particular highlight for me was a few months later when, sat with friends Phil and H on the stylish bar stools contemplating the night ahead, I spotted a familiar baseball capped figure walk behind me towards the toilets. I only managed to catch a glimpse of him from the back as he walked away from the bar but I was quite sure it was who I thought it was.

I eagerly awaited his re-emergence from the amenities to confirm my thoughts. I greeted the legend that was Mr Danny Tenaglia as he rounded the corner of the bar area towards me. He was headlining Steve Lawler's night at Code.

"How did you guess it was me?" he said in his soft New York drawl.

"The hat and the smile gave it away", I replied as his grin widened beyond Cheshire Cat proportions.

Much to our delight, he spent the next 10 minutes chatting with us about various projects he had been working on over the last year. I enthused about his New York protégé Celeda, whose album Danny has produced. He was very grateful for my comments and acknowledged my apparent wealth of knowledge about his work.

He continued to inform me about his most recent work with Eighties legends Depeche Mode who had recently released their new album 'Exciter'. His remix of the much vaunted *I Feel Loved* he described to me as a '14-minute monster', and boy was he right!

Back to the night of our first visit to the club, and as Sasha's arrival was imminent we excitedly rushed through the main entrance, each adorned with our silver VIP wristbands.

We made our way up the steep, space age stairway with its discreet lights housed in the stairs. The futuristic theme continued as I reached

God is a DJ*

the heavy double doors at the top of the stairs that made the sound from the club barely audible from outside. On opening the doors the bass frequencies hit you like a hammer and we were still a good distance from the centre of the dance floor, which was on the level below. This only whetted our appetites even more for what was to come.

Steve Lawler was playing a classic remix of Depeche Mode's *It's No Good* and Dave Gahan's vocals floated crystal clear over the thumping bass. I looked tentatively over the steel mesh barrier down at the dance floor. Early signs were promising, as a good number had already taken up their positions for the night at their respective corners of the main arena whilst the podium-cum-catwalk which ran from the back of the dance floor into the middle had a shape throwing contest already under way.

We took in the new surroundings, looking upwards giving the impression of tourists in New York as we strained our necks to get a view of who was sitting in the booths that filled the upper balcony surrounding the dance floor.

We ventured upstairs for a better view of what the club had to offer and predictably found all the booths already taken up by eager clubbers warming to sonorous beats just below. We returned to our original spot an hour later to find the head count had doubled. As we struggled for standing room near the main bar, I wondered where the VIP wristbands would lead us.

Another set of steel double doors, situated at the side of the first floor bar area, had an accompanying large member of security, always a good sign that something of interest would be behind them. As we approached him, he clocked our wristbands and gratefully opened the door to reveal another similarly fashioned staircase to the one we had just come up.

As I reached the top of these stairs, the thud of the PA system in the club began to fade at the same time as the familiar chugging beats of Dirty Vegas's *Days Go By* came into earshot. We followed the beats, spellbound like children of the Pied Piper, into what was a whole other party happening directly above the salient dance floor below.

This was and still is the best VIP room I've yet to encounter, from the sweeping slate bar that accommodates a sunken set of Technics turntables and mixer to the cool, cream leather, modular seating area.

Most of the seats were already taken up with music industry types, glamour pusses and DJ wannabes, all busy talking the talk, whilst we nestled in nicely at the bar, clocking a few familiar faces whilst waiting to be served. Heads nodded to the cool beats of bar resident for the night Marc Cohen, who originates from Manchester. He now resides at Steve Lawler's own successful monthly 'Harlem Nights' at the End in London.

The music could comfortably be heard above the spontaneous banter that otherwise filled the room, right up until 'the man like' walked through the doors. He was running late as usual and so didn't get chance to stop and chat as he was going on in 15 minutes, but the reaction just went to confirm his fame as a DJ.

Walking down a busy shopping street on a Saturday afternoon and hardly anyone would know he's there, yet transport him to any club in the country and the room becomes hushed at his arrival.

A quick acknowledgement to the people he recognised was all he had time for before he took over from resident Lawler, who had been entertaining the escalating crowd with his staple brand of dirty house music. This dark, sonorous introduction of sounds to the night was perfect for the stark landscape of such a huge club to host, with moody lighting to complement.

The place was now rammed to capacity and it hadn't yet reached midnight. Sasha's absence from Birmingham for more than two years had only heightened expectations for the 'concrete capital' crowd who were now baying for him to make the new arena come alive with his magic.

I had negotiated the correct listening position in a club ie the centre of the dance floor, by way of pushing, squeezing and sidling past the hordes that now packed onto the floor. Even at the ripe old age of 31, I still got that excited feeling when the last record of the previous DJ beats out before Sasha takes over and the rumblings of his first track seamlessly flow out from the speakers.

These were no ordinary speakers though. Before the opening of such a major club, the management team knew they had to take the sound and lighting a stage further than most clubs in the UK had dared previously. They were aiming for a huge, clean sound to fill the vast rectangular room that would 'make your clothes shake yet you could still hold a conversation'.

God is a DJ*

It was a tall order but made possible by the introduction of eight enormous JBL custom built speakers banked on the sides of the dance floor with an array of tweeters above for that extra sonic effect. The resulting sound was so encapsulating it was as though you were listening through a pair of headphones whilst the bass bins pounded your rib cage.

Sasha's first record sets the tone for the rest of his set with a powerfully emotional track that seeps into your bones with haunting, swirling strings and the heartrending thud of a bassline. It's a grand statement that he has arrived.

From the moment that first record had been effortlessly mixed into the next, the dance floor remained a constant throng of ardent Sasha fans spellbound by his magic, highlighted by Minimalistix's *Struggle for Pleasure*, a contradiction in terms if ever there was one.

Three dreamlike hours later, having been captivated in a vacuum of sexy, percussive rhythms, we had reached the peak of his set with Bedrock's 'Voices' creeping out of the PA system with the subtly of a kitten but roaring like a lion at its zenith. Then the familiar ascending stabs of synth from Trisco's *Muzak* began to build and the rapturous crowd responded in time to the break as the bassline thundered out.

The journey that had unravelled with a compulsive energy and technical brilliance was almost at an end as Sasha interrupted the music momentarily. This focused the crowd's attention even more intently than before and their perseverance was rewarded when he demonstrated his prodigious production talents with the echoing synth intro to his all-conquering *Xpander* track that has graced so many an unforgettable night since it was first played out.

Needless to say, the raptures with which it was received meant a moment etched indelibly in people's minds. Again!

11

Tribal Sessions

Sankeys Soap, Manchester, 2001–2003

'AND on the seventh day God created Manchester' was a term born out of the early acid house days from 1988 when clubs like the Haçienda and Konspiracy exploded into life.

This period also spawned a creative flow from locally based bands such as The Stone Roses, Happy Mondays and Inspiral Carpets to name but a few, who all enjoyed enormous chart success and quickly built up hardcore followings leading to sell out gigs up and down the country. 'Madchester', as it became known, had a new breed of young kids dressed in baggy jeans, psychedelic hooded tops and brightly coloured kicker boots or suede wallabies, eager to embrace this new found culture.

Manchester was already established as one of the leading cities in the UK in respect of being a forerunner of music and fashion before this latest explosion. The early part of the unfashionable Eighties had already produced massive bands like The Smiths and more importantly for me, New Order.

I was eager with anticipation when they announced in 2000 that they were to produce a new album and undertake a UK tour to accompany it after being out of the limelight for more than six years. The particular Friday in October 2001 when they played their home city again was set to be a night to welcome home Manchester's prodigal sons.

However it wasn't only New Order who would be playing in the city that night. Sankeys Soap had also booked the return of another folklore hero, Sasha, who was playing Manchester for the first time in four years.

Sankeys' weekly Friday night 'Tribal Sessions' had quickly established itself as the premier night in the country for progressive tribal beats with the aid of rising star Greg Vickers, who was installed as resident. Alongside, a who's who of dance music made regularly

God is a DJ*

appearances, including Steve Lawler, Layo and Bushwacka, John Digweed and Deep Dish to name but a few.

This was some feat, as just over five years earlier Sankeys Soap was just another disused club space having suffered from the backlash of gangs and crime that had spread through the heart of the city's once thriving clubland like a virus.

The infamous Gallery nightclub was the first to succumb to Manchester's gun law in 1989. Its closure led to gangs heading for a new venue to hang out, and they found it in the shape of the Haçienda where the fight for control of the door would continue for almost a decade before the inevitable end of its existence in 1997.

In this period, the lesser known cavernous club Konspiracy, formerly known as Pips, came under threat after persistent stolen door takings became the norm until the police revoked its licence in the spring of 1991 after only six months trading. The aptly named 'Most Excellent' followed suit in the summer of 1992 after the entrance to its home at Millionaire's nightclub, renamed Wiggly Worm, was ram-raided.

The problems culminated in running battles inside the Haçienda's main rival, Home nightclub, by 40 or so balaclava-clad gangsters, leaving authorities with no option but to close it down. Only Sankeys Soap remained, running its successful 'Golden' and 'Bugged Out' nights under the guidance of Andy Spiro and John Hill, before it too eventually succumbed.

It wasn't until two brave promoters-cum-pioneers, namely Sacha Lord-Marchionne and Dave Vincent, decided to join forces as opposed to competing against each other for a monopoly of the city's lesser-known club nights, that Sankeys would be resurrected.

Sacha ran a popular student night in Manchester at Paradise Factory whereas Dave had been doing one-off events up and down the country. I asked Sacha how their paths crossed and whose brave idea it was to re-open Sankeys.

> *On that rival thing, it turned out one day we were chatting on the phone and I forget what we were talking about but I had to rush off to get my wife Elisa's birthday present, he said.*
>
> *Dave asked me: 'Well, when's her birthday then?' and I told him 6th October. 'Oh fucking hell,' he said. 'That's Patsy's birthday.' She was his girlfriend at the time. And he then asked: 'What's*

your birthday?' and I said 26th January, and there was a deadly silence. That was Dave's birthday as well, so something sort of clicked.

We were trying to do a monthly event at the Academy in Manchester. We booked a meeting with the guy there, Sean Morgan. Dave came up from London but Sean never turned up. He was pissed from the night before. So he apologised, and we rearranged it for the following week. Again Dave came all the way from London and Sean didn't turn up again, so we said 'Right, fuck him. We're not going to do the Academy, forget that.'

We were really pissed off, trying to think of another venue, but there were no other venues that had created the kind of vibe of what we wanted to do, and to be honest, the Academy wasn't ideal but it was the best of a bad bunch.

Then I got a call from Dave at about six in the morning. He said: 'Listen, are you sat down?' I said: 'Yeah, I'm in bed. Why?'

'I've got this crazy idea, I've not been able to sleep all night. Why don't you, me and John Hill try to reopen Sankeys?'

John Hill owned Golden at the time, which had run successfully for a time at Sankeys before its closure.

I said: 'Dave, it's not going to happen, there's no way. The police have objected to everyone who's tried to open it. It would be an amazing venue I know but we're just not going to get it.'

Obviously there were issues of the previous Sankeys and the way it was run so I thought it was a long shot, probably one in a hundred chance of doing it, but I made an appointment with the police who were always impressed at nights I'd done previously.

I met with Daryl Butterworth, a licensing officer for the police, who said: 'Look, I advise you not to do it, you are going to have all sorts of problems so I suggest you stick to your student night.'

I told him how determined we were to do this and how much we wanted it to work, so we had to go away and come back with a

God is a DJ*

> *proposal with a full presentation to the police, and in the end we kind of semi got them on board.*
>
> *In fact the day we got our licence, one of the magistrates was heard by our solicitors saying to one of his colleagues: 'I can't believe Sankeys Soap has re-opened. No one thought it would actually happen again.'*
>
> *The warning from the police that day was 'You'll only see the blue lights once and when you see them, that's your last night – one warning and that's it!'*
>
> *But we managed to put into practice full CCTVs and a proper door team to the point where we are now blowing our own trumpet and they now use us as an example of how a club should be run in Manchester, which is very comforting to know.*

The plan wasn't without its doubters as Sankeys was situated in one of the 'dead' parts of town, in a place called Ancoats, littered with disused warehouses and derelict housing estates. I had never been to Sankeys the first time it was open. Maybe one of the reasons was its implausible location but somehow it was a night I missed off my list of clubs to go to.

For Sacha and Dave to have confidence in people wanting to venture out into the unknown recesses of Ancoats was a brave move to say the least. When asked if he was worried about reopening the club in such a run-down area, his confidence surprised me somewhat.

> *If Sankeys was on Deansgate or was in the Printworks, somewhere like that, you wouldn't get the vibe you are after because the club would just be full of beer monsters who weren't there to appreciate the music, he said.*
>
> *The fact that it is a destination venue is important, the customers who are coming through the doors are there for the right reasons. The people who are making that extra five minute walk from the centre of town to the venue are here for the music. They know what they're talking about and it's the sort of venue that they would want to go to.*
>
> *If we were at the Printworks, in the Village or anywhere else in town, it simply wouldn't work for us. Don't get me wrong, we'd*

probably make a lot more money, because we'd be sold out every single night, but it would be the wrong crowd we were attracting and not what we wanted to achieve.

The nearest public house to the club, and I use the term public house very loosely, is 'The Dead Arms', as I affectionately refer to it. My first experience of this establishment was on the coldest night in the history of the world, New Year's Eve 2000.

I had sorted tickets out for everyone as usual and handed them out to all 28 of us in the foyer of the Jury's Inn, on the opposite side of town from Sankeys, where we were all staying. It was a great turn out and the first New Year's Eve I was to spend with my brother Chris, 10 years my junior.

Taxis had been booked well in advance to take us all from the hotel to Sankeys at around 10.30pm, but it seemed word had already got out that we would be arriving at that time as the queue was snaking out of sight when we pulled up at the entrance.

To avoid turning blue, we decided to have a swift few in the 'Dead Arms' next door and let the queue die down. A pub with no visible front door is never a good sign, especially in the harsh throes of winter, but there was music blaring out onto the street and a light on so at least there were some signs of life inside.

As the whole crew of us entered the pub, the expression on our faces was one of bewilderment as we noted the décor had deteriorated somewhat, with large hammer-shaped holes in most walls and ceiling tiles strategically hanging precariously overhead. The girls in particular were less than impressed, as they were dressed in high-heeled strappy shoes and best dresses and didn't exactly blend into the surroundings.

The boys' first impressions were soon forgotten when a friendly middle-aged man behind the bar, who I presumed to be the landlord, welcomed us with a free shot to warm our cockles. No signs of draught beer though, or a till register. Just a fridge full of canned lager and cider and a Tupperware box for his takings. I didn't bother to ask if he took Switch or did cash back. This was taking minimalism to the extreme but it was better than standing queuing in perishing cold outside. Not that it was any warmer indoors, but at least we had a drink in our hands.

God is a DJ*

The gap in the market for somewhere credible to go to before entering the club is something owners Sasha and Dave are very aware of.

> We actually looked at a couple of pre-club bars including one on Tib Street called Centro, said Sasha. We had an interest in that but it was too expensive.

> We have got plans to open next door but we'll wait until the area is a bit more established and redeveloped. Within 12 months this area will have a lot of residents round here so we'll probably open the bar then, but at the moment I don't think it would work here. We already do lots of pre-club warm ups at places like Loaf and Revolution.

In stark contrast to New Year's Eve, that Friday night when New Order were playing at the Apollo and Sasha was back in town was one of those hazy, warm Indian summer evenings that we are now so accustomed to in early October.

All the males wore short sleeves or less while the women gave a great display of bare backs and navels, much to our delight. Taxi ranks were idle as nobody minded walking to their destination and most of the 'working men's' public houses in Salford had white plastic chairs outside their entrances to entice the occasional passer-by to sample their best bitter whilst taking in the traffic fumes on the pavement.

Of the 15 of us who had tickets for New Order, only six were to continue the night at Sankeys for such a rare appearance by Sasha. We had all decided to get the train into town at around 7pm so as to make the most of the evening with a swift few drinks in the Revolution bar on Oxford Road. This part of town is Manchester's main student area and the place was still busy with those stretching out their afternoon into early hours of the evening. This was obvious from the noise coming from a party in the far corner of the bar, whose lectures I presumed had finished at around lunchtime.

The gig started at 9pm, leaving plenty of time to enjoy a few more drinks, some playful banter and the cool, laid back sounds of the resident DJ who mixed acid jazz with hip-hop and house. An unexpectedly nice start to the evening and it wasn't even nine o'clock.

It's not too difficult to find a cab around this early hour and so we split into three groups, all flagging down a black cab each within seconds of each other. Arriving fashionably late, much to my dismay, we entered the venue just as the last bars of *Crystal*, New Order's anthemic opening track and my favourite from their latest album, was fading out.

I wasn't disheartened for too long though as they powered through many of theirs and my favourite tracks from their back catalogue. An acid house remake of *Bizarre Love Triangle*, the legendary *Touched by the Hand of God* sung verbatim by the sold-out crowd and the majestic *True Faith* were the highlights, whilst the haunting *Love Will Tear us Apart* and *Atmosphere* from the Joy Division era rounded off an epic set that will be talked about for years to come.

New Order are renowned for never doing an encore, but seeing as they were playing in their hometown for the first time since they were at the Nynex Arena in 1999, it was only appropriate to give the packed house what they deserved. The opening chords to *Blue Monday* resonated round the place as the hardcore fans at the front of the stage showered each other with drinks and armpits.

The more sedate among us stood at the side of the lighting and sound booth, more than happy to make our own party for what may be the last time the band ever toured. But then again, you never know.

A large vocal contingent applauded and beckoned for one more but the only thing left for New Order to do was bow and take the rapturous applause they so richly deserved. A sweating Bernard Sumner gave a swift "Thank you and good night Manchester" and promptly left the stage with the sound of Hooky's bass guitar reverberating next to the speaker.

As people dispersed into the street, we quickly regrouped outside, poignantly confirming to each other how good the band had actually been, evoking memories of the first time I had heard the 'Substance' and 'Technique' albums as a bright-eyed teenager. Those are memories to share with your siblings just like my dad tells me about the Northern Soul scene and gigs featuring Motown legends who always sang live, not like the rubbish today.

It was now approaching 11pm and I was aware that Sasha would be starting his set at Sankeys at around midnight. I knew this having spoken to him earlier on in the day at the Malmaison Hotel, where he was staying for the night. It was noticeable in the tone of his voice that he was genuinely excited about his return to Manchester, but nonetheless it wasn't without a lot of endeavour from 'the other

Sacha' and Dave that he had been persuaded to return to his 'home town'. The former explained to me their masterplan to get Sasha to play at his club.

> Yes, obviously Sasha was a name that we wanted but when we first opened the club we had to prove to him that it was a venue worthy of him playing, he said.
>
> The problem was that when we first opened, it was hard to get the DJs that we wanted. Like Sasha for example. He just wouldn't come here straight away, so we had to prove ourselves to all the agents and if you look at our first bookings, they weren't big crowd pullers.
>
> It was Dave that actually stalked him and this isn't a joke. Dave literally stalked him for weeks and weeks, turning up at all his gigs, trying to pitch him and pitch him.
>
> In the end we found out he had a weak spot for Haçienda memorabilia. Some of our lights are the original Haçienda lights with the Haçienda logo on the side of them, so we took one down, bubble wrapped it, stuck Dave and Greg in a car and sent them all the way up to Scotland to one of Sasha's gigs at the Arches.
>
> He was completely overcome with our gesture and agreed to do the gig. Later on though in an interview in the Manchester Evening News said he only agreed to do it to get rid of his stalker!

I'd agreed to see Sasha inside the club and confirmed our names on his guest list. Sankeys was a good 20-minute walk away so we joined the masses that had decided to march towards town, eager to catch a post-gig pint or continue onto a club until the early hours. As we approached Piccadilly, the six of us bade our farewells to the rest of the party not fortunate enough to be going to Sankeys and headed up Oldham Street towards our destination.

Jersey Street, where the club is situated, is quite a long, winding desolate street off a busy carriageway that cuts into the city centre of Manchester. On turning into it there are no apparent signs of life, leaving strangers to the area wondering whether someone has given them duff information about the club's whereabouts.

I have probably been asked the same question, ie whether I have heard of a club called Sankeys, at the same spot more than 50 times. Each time the questioner reluctantly follows me round the first bend until there appears a chink of light halfway down the street, much to their relief. The seamless stream of taxis that pass you by, particularly on a night when Sasha is playing, also boosts confidence of its vicinity.

The dimly lit queue of people also quickly comes into view, though I'm lucky enough to be on the right hand side of door where the lovely Elisa stands with her trusty clipboard. Unfortunately the wire fencing that shields her from the jostling crowds does not deflect or prevent Manchester's blustery weather from leaving her feeling numb with windburn after three hours ticking names off the list. Husband and co-owner Sacha usually does the honours of greeting and walking us through to the club, leaving his poor wife with teeth chattering at the entrance. Still, he always makes sure she's well wrapped up in a nice coat.

The entrance to Sankeys is a large cobbled path under an archway, and it can prove quite hazardous on a freezing night with girls in high shoes doing their impressions of Bambi on Ice. As you walk clear of the archway, immediately on your left is one of the many outbuildings that houses the only outdoor cloakroom in clubland.

Entry to the club is adjacent to this, through a dark double doorway with only one of the security staff giving it away, apart from the fact that the interior doors visibly shudder from the thundering bass bins hidden behind them. The main speakers fill the recesses of the main dance floor from floor to ceiling and the sound easily fills the long, narrow room with its low ceiling, giving that intimate feel for all who step through the doors.

As music was the priority for the club to achieve its success, the importance of the right sound system was paramount. If they were to entice the biggest DJs in the world to play here, then they needed a sound system to match. When the green light was received from the authorities to go ahead with reopening Sankeys, the issue needed to be addressed immediately.

When we first opened, we didn't have a pot to piss in so we had to rent a sound system, which was a good one. I think it was called the 'ASS' or something but it was decent because it had to be as Sankeys was all about the music, said Sacha.

We knew we couldn't skip corners by hiring a cheap sound system, so the guy we were hiring it from, Pete Dyer, phoned Dave one day in the office and said: 'Listen, Home in Leicester Square has gone bust, and they've got a sound system there called the Phazon.'

Dave had always been a big fan of the Phazon and before we got this phone call, Dave had flown across to New York to see the inventor of it, Steve Dash, to price one up for the club. He reckoned once we'd installed it and flown him across a few times, we were looking at between £150 and £160k. There was no way we could afford that kind of money, it was impossible. So when we got this phone call by chance, offering us Home's system for sale, we were really interested. It was between us and Space in Ibiza. Our offer was a lot less but because we could buy it straight away and the receivers wanted a quick turnaround, we got it.

Problem was, we were that excited, we never measured it or anything like that. Now if you walk into Sankeys and look at the pipes, it's made it by about four millimetres, it scrapes in. Those pipes are essential to the whole water system so couldn't be moved. When the guy turned up to fit it he just said: 'This isn't gonna fit into the club.' But we made him install it into the club to prove him wrong.

Since we got the system, Sasha has claimed it to be the best system in the UK. I mean Sasha makes the Phazon in a way. I think with that system you have to understand it and he does better than anyone.

The DJ booth is right where it should be, in the middle of the club, to the right hand side of the dance floor, although where the floor starts and ends is immaterial because when the music's right, the whole place is engulfed in a fervent, electrifying atmosphere that defies anyone not to feel part of it.

To the side of the DJ booth, which is made of brick, possibly to make the DJ feel at home, is the staircase to the Soap Bar. This usually houses different local promoters, from breaks crews like Airtight, who have recently secured a residency for Friday nights, to the more housier Redlight on Saturday night with the likes of Angel Deelite and, I'm proud to say, my very own night Ace of Clubs.

Having been a regular since Sankeys reopened its doors, if you would have asked me to pick any club in the country to put a night on I would have chosen Sankeys every time, such has been my passion for this resurrection of Manchester clubland.

Along with mates and co-promoters Gareth and Warby, who is also our resident DJ, we were thrilled to be asked by Sacha if we would be interested in joining forces with Sankeys to enable our members to sample the delights of such a great night. Not needing to be asked twice, we jumped at the chance to host the upstairs Soap Bar for three months preceding Christmas.

Our second visit in November even bettered our debut gig as not only was Danny Rampling playing downstairs but Danny Tenaglia, who was booked to play at the club the following night for a scheduled 10 hour marathon, decided to have sneak preview of the venue. He walked up the stairs to find his and fortunately one of our favourites, T-Connection's *At Midnight*, just beating in with its extended percussive disco rhythms. Promoter Sacha pulled me to the side of the booth to inform me of his arrival but just like Darth Vader had told Luke Skywalker how he knew what he had got for Christmas, I had already felt his presence.

Events such as the legendary story of George Best lying on a king size hotel bed strewn with money, a naked Miss World next to him and buckets of champagne on the table and the porter asking him: "Where did it all go wrong, George?" are now folklore history. And similarly, each time Sasha plays in Manchester it becomes part of the city's chronicles. The atmosphere is nothing short of electric, and both Sacha the promoter and I agree wholeheartedly on the impact he has when he arrives in town.

> *I think it's different when Sasha plays here because it's almost creating history, isn't it? said Sacha.*
>
> *He's like a legend and though obviously very big names play at the club like Carl Cox and Pete Tong, because of Sasha's Manchester roots and his early northern residencies when he returns it's like winding the clock back 10 years.*

God is a DJ*

The crowd of 10 years ago comes back together with the new kids who've read about it and want to experience the night. Literally the second the doors open, the place fills up and by the time he walks in, the place is rammed and arms are in the air. Sasha could stand in the DJ booth, get his cock out and not even play a record and everyone would have their arms in the air!

I must say the last statement is probably true although how long he could hold that pose, I couldn't say.

Although I have been fortunate to be present at many a Sasha night, each appearance he has made at Sankeys has always been someone's 'first time' and the expectation felt in the room is very infectious to the point where you could almost pick out the 'virgins' by their excitable demeanour.

On his first appearance on that hazy Indian summer night of 2001, I could have probably been mistaken as a first timer such was my enthusiasm, even though I had seen him the month before in Ibiza for his birthday. Arriving at the venue at around 11pm, the queues were reminiscent of the Christmas sale at Next, the difference being that most of the blokes in this queue were actually looking forward to getting inside.

Fortunately we were ushered in on the right hand side, courtesy of Mrs Lord-Marchionne, who handed our wristbands through the wire mesh fencing that protected the entrance.

At around this time on a regular night, you enter the venue, go past the girl on the till, and as you open the double doors the first thing that hits you is the wall of sound. Once your ears have adjusted to the sudden rise in decibels and your heart beat returns to a resting state, you can usually wander across the dancefloor towards the downstairs bar.

However, on the night Sasha played we were met with a wall of bodies already packed into the venue at this early hour. We fought our way through the initial crowd towards the bar area at the rear of the club for a few swift vodka liveners before the main event got under way.

Greg Vickers, the Tribal Sessions resident, had the BPMs powering through the Phazon system with some trademark tribal beats to get the swelling crowd moving their feet.

As the anticipation reached fever pitch, a few people near the DJ booth pre-empted Sasha's imminent arrival with whistles. This gave a false alarm for clubbers out of sight of the rear doors where Sasha would make his appearance a full 30 minutes later. Most started to cheer and prematurely celebrate his arrival, which only heightened the tension in the club even more.

This exercise was repeated twice before 12.15 when the rear doors opened and Sasha strode in to what you can only describe as pandemonium. It was at this point I was well aware that some people around me had only heard rumours of the mighty Sasha, checking with others stood next to them to confirm the bloke with the white T-shirt and head bowed really was the 'Son of God'.

Sasha's thoughts on such moments are encapsulated as follows.

You feel the energy of the crowd and the buzz when you walk in that room, the adrenaline level is so high. Sometimes I get back to the hotel and I'm so exhausted I wake up in my clothes and think 'What the fuck happened?'

The moment the needle touched the vinyl set the tone for the night as a murky, driving bass spewed out of the speakers. It was hands in the air time from the first beats of his set and with every confidence the night would continue in this vein, you couldn't help but smile. This was what Manchester had been waiting so long for.

As the night progressed, we set up camp for the early part of his set near the bar. The passing traffic of people between dance floor, toilet and bar was relentless as was the amount of familiar faces from Shelley's and the Haç who acknowledged each other with a confident, cognizant bow of the head.

As the pulsing beats intensified, you were almost coaxed nearer the main action on the dance floor without noticing, like your feet had a mind of their own. Before we knew it, we were stood in our favourite spot in front of the lighting man Graham, who looks old enough to be my grandad, although I very much doubt Sankeys would really be my grandad's bag.

This small space at the bottom of the stairs is where I've experienced many a memorable night in the presence of Tribal legend Steve Lawler and Redlight favourites Tom and Andy of Groove Armada. Each are deserving of their own mention for the unique experience they have brought to this now Mecca of the North.

God is a DJ*

However none come close to the atmosphere created when Sasha graces the decks. His set began to build when a soundscape of deep house fused a pulsing, whirring breakbeat that seamlessly melted into the melodic opening beats of Depeche Mode's *Freelove*, with Dave Gahan's haunting vocal searing through the PA system.

Although a brand new track to most ears, by the break of the second verse its new familiarity to the crowd was astonishing, such is its instant hookline of 'no hidden catch, no strings attached, just free love!' The consequential lights, courtesy of our friend Graham, responded in time with the break in the record and illuminated the whole club as arms once again reached for the stars.

As the night unfolded with a pace equal to that at which the Manchester skyline is expanding in this age when there is an obsession to build on any fallow terra firma, we noticed it was already 2.30am. I was very much aware that the last hour of magic was already in progress but as with all Sasha nights, things were only going to get better.

His understanding of Sankeys' Phazon system enables him to put it through its paces whilst putting the crowd through their full range of emotions. His set was etched with sizzling breakbeats and twisted house through to the driving progressive sounds of Funk D'Void's *Diabla*.

The club descended momentarily into darkness bar the pulsing strobe light, intensifying everyone's senses as Sasha retained his usual composed stance in the confines of the esoteric DJ booth. His concentrated pose then burst into life when he played an unknown track that turned out to be the now massive *Take Me With You* by Cosmos. The opening bars are a basic synth bleep that gradually picks up pace followed by the simplest of basslines. The track then builds with the whooshing sound of a jumbo jet taking off before it breaks. From this moment, the whole place went into a state of pandemonium and as I said before, when Sasha jumps, everybody jumps. The lights reacted in sync with the break of the record and the strobe faded into a kaleidoscope of reds and blues reminiscent of an Aurora Borealis scene.

I phoned him on the Sunday night, having taken two days and a game of football to return to normality. The name of the track was requested on a 'need to know basis' as it had made such an impact from first time hearing, particularly as I had received three text messages myself asking its title. Sasha only knew it was by Cosmos, aka producer/artist Tom Middleton, and for the time being had called it '1980'.

During our Sunday evening chat Sasha sought reassurance regarding the way he played. This self-doubt proved just how humble and modest he portrays himself at times. I in turn just laughed and asked if this was a trick question as I had never seen such a reaction since Shelley's in its heyday during the summer of 1990.

Having reached fever pitch in Sankeys, it was left to round the night off with his signature tune. This time though it was *Xpander* with a twist as it was mixed seamlessly with Underworld's *Cowgirl*. The track is so subtle yet the emotional impact it had on the dance floor was devastating.

As the spiralling, twisted intro intensified, the crowd absorbed the cacophony of noise as *Xpander Girl* kicked into life for a full 10 minutes that transported everyone into a state of euphoria. The ovation that followed was of presidential status as the crowd remained whistling and clapping in the harsh, bright main lights that brought everyone back to reality.

It would be almost 12 months before Sasha returned to his adopted home to promote the release of his debut album *Airdrawndagger*.

Following years of rumours and speculation, it took a strange twist of fate that would enable him to concentrate his efforts solely on completing his seminal album.

Just before the 2001 Winter Music Conference in Miami, Sasha had an unfortunate road accident in a taxi, leaving him with a perforated eardrum. Forbidden from flying and unable to listen to any noises above the sound of church mice meant his usual globe-trotting lifestyle was curtailed for the foreseeable future. Yet instead of wallowing in self-pity Sasha decided to utilise his unscheduled vacation to the full.

> *I hadn't taken my foot off the gas since I started DJing 12 years ago, Sasha told Radio 1. I really needed to take some time off to finish the album. The accident forced me to slow down for a while and gave me the opportunity to write some songs, which ultimately allowed me to finish the album. I signed a deal to make this record eight years ago, but even after I completed Xpander; I still felt that I needed to learn my way around the*

God is a DJ*

> studio. I wanted to make a record that was truly mine, and to do that, I felt I needed to know how to use the equipment in my studio. But when you spend most of your time travelling as a DJ, you don't have the time you need to learn everything.
>
> It's been difficult for me to take the time off to make an album. I didn't really want to spend time in the studio, to be honest. I completely focused on my DJing. I spent four-and-a-half years playing at Twilo every month, and every time I did that, it would take a week out of my calendar. Then there were my gigs in the rest of the world.
>
> I really enjoyed being out there DJing, and I would take a month off here or there to work on music. The most I ever took off was two months, thinking I'd get my album done, but you can't write an album in two fucking months — well, I can't anyway.

Once his mind was set on completing the album, the writing for each track flowed quickly and within three weeks of the accident, the majority of the writing was done. He had started writing earlier material with long-time friend Charlie May, of Spooky fame, back in 1997. However he soon realised that to capture the sound he wanted would require a little help from his friends.

> I hooked up with Tom Holkenborg from Junkie XL, he said. Tom took a lot of the ideas that Charlie and I had been working on over the last three years and made them sound like album tracks. Suddenly we had four or five tracks together, and we were in the zone. I was ready to get on with it.
>
> I spent several months in Amsterdam finishing up the production side of things and doing some more writing. From writing to mixing, it took about 10 months of work for me to complete this album, which I feel is pretty normal. A couple of the tracks were written several years ago when William Orbit asked us to do some demos for Madonna. We kept a couple of them for ourselves. Charlie and I have been working together for about five years and we've done a load of tracks. While there are 11 tracks on the album, there are another 40 that didn't make it.

The other musketeer was sound designer Simon Wright, who took charge of much of the album's design as well as constantly surprising both Sasha and Charlie with completely new sounds he'd invented by passing them through what Sasha calls his 'analogue washing machine'. As a production team, he feels they have a strong, solid base, likening their partnership in the studio with that of his and John Digweed's as DJs.

Those with preconceptions about how the album would turn out were somewhat dumbfounded that he didn't go for an all-out assault on the dance floor in an *Xpander* type of way, but as he explained the ideology behind the concept of making an album, you began to understand where he was coming from.

> *I wanted to make an album that was listenable on different levels: at home, on the way to the club, after the club. I didn't want to make something that only worked in a club environment. There are a few tracks on the album that do work in a club, but the record's atmosphere and sound make it accessible at home as well. I've always loved epic, atmospheric music like Future Sound of London, The Orb or Leftfield, whose 'Leftism' is a very cinematic album. That really got under my skin. It's taken me 10 years to follow in their footsteps, but I've always aspired to create that kind of sound.*

When listening to the album at home with friends, the complex melodies and sweeping string sections come to the fore, letting you immerse yourself in such an idyllic soundscape, yet when hearing the same tracks played out in a club, they possess a far more intense resonance.

The time Danny Tenaglia played one of the more up-tempo tracks from the album, 'Cloud Cuckoo', in Sankeys remains fond in my memory. That was not only because of the fact that he chose to play it out but because the all-encompassing bassline that dominated the track had not been so obvious in the comfort of my living room and I thought it was his own remix.

After most gigs he plays, Sasha usually seeks reassurance on his set. However, after playing Sankeys at his album launch night and road testing a number of tracks from the album he was positively buoyant, the completion of his album giving him a renewed confidence.

> *I feel like I finally have a solid foundation under me, he said. Before I finished* Airdrawndagger, *I never felt complete. I was*

God is a DJ*

always playing someone else's music or remixing someone else's tune. Now I feel like I can really call myself an artist. This album feels a bit more grown-up than my other work.

Spoken like a fully grown up DJ.

12

Circus

Masque, Liverpool, June 2005

IN the last 20 years, I have been fortunate to see Sasha evolve, from humble clubber to pin up DJ, to sought after remixer, then to established artist in his own right, culminating with the release of his long awaited debut album *Airdrawndagger*.

The progression has been a steady yet arduous one with a touch of good fortune but a great deal of hard work, not to mention seeing the world in the process. Not one to complain, Sasha is always aware of the charmed life he leads. When he was in his five-star hotel in LA during the 'Airdrawndagger' tour, I spoke to him from my unassuming office situated near his one-time residence in Salford, Manchester.

"It's going really well but the tour is taking its toll on me physically and mentally," he told me in an English accent surprisingly untarnished considering the amount of time he's spent in the States over the past decade.

His home he now considers as New York, for the time being, where he has lived with his new wife Zoië for the past four years. However, his punishing schedule has meant it has been used as little more than a base due to lengthy periods of time in Amsterdam completing the album as well as his annual excursions to Ibiza, not to mention Asia and Australia.

The album was very well received by most critics and most importantly his peers.

> I expected a mixed review just because it wasn't like Xpander, but that was relevant to that period of my life. Even those who've had a go at it still have something positive to say so it's all good. But the people I have most respect for all sent me personal messages which meant a great deal to me.

The hype that preceded its release was one reminiscent of a Spielberg movie for those in the music industry and the quotes that followed were of equal proportion.

God is a DJ*

A collection of beautiful music from the heart of Sasha, nothing short of brilliant – A gorgeous expansion of the melodic dance music – An overwhelming sense of sophistication and control – Airdrawndagger *grows and breathes as if alive.*

The superlatives continued and it was obvious that Sasha had taken a big step forward in the evolution of dance music to make people sit up and take such notice. I asked him what the next step was after the tour ends.

I've got to get away with Zoië to a place where we can escape and spend some quality time together but after that I'll probably do a few gigs back in New York and LA where I've got a few projects in the pipeline.

I wondered if DJing would be enough to satiate his appetite for all things new now that he had taken his skills that step further. After all, he had already had some success in other avenues after being asked to write the music for Sony Playstation's biggest game release of 1999, 'Wipeout 3'.

He said the idea of scoring a soundtrack to a film carried huge appeal. His close friend Brian Transeau has already completed scores for the blockbuster 'Fast and Furious' as well as the less hyped 'Go' by the director of 'Swingers'. Having dipped his toe into the entertainment world and spent a considerable time in Los Angeles, it is only a matter of time before the right offer proves too much to resist and his first score is completed.

Being one of the few who were largely responsible for the meteoric rise in DJ culture through the Nineties that saw turntables outsell guitars by four to one, Sasha's mystique was one of wonderment and awe. Bedroom DJs would spend hours sourcing his chart returns, pursuing rare vinyl like hunters chased tigers for trophies in Africa. And by the turn of the millennium, most kids with a pair of decks could beat match to perfection, and so the aura surrounding the magic DJ bubble had burst.

Australian website Resident Advisor quizzed Sasha on the changes afoot.

There was something magical about the performances, he said. Then everybody and their uncle suddenly got a pair of decks and figured it all out, and the mystery that made the shows interesting slowly disappeared.

Ten years is a long time in the world of technology and vinyl was taking a hammering from the digital revolution with CDs and now MP3s. As Sasha told Yuri Wuensch of Ibiza Voice website, he fought the transition for as long as possible before relenting.

I was one of the last people to switch over to CDs, he said, adding that early DJ CD players like the first Pioneer CDJ-1000 simply weren't up to snuff.

It felt horrible. I remember trying to play out with it and I kept making mistakes. Because of that, I didn't automatically jump on it.

His protégé James Zabiela, a good 10 years his junior, had already grasped Pioneer's CDJs with both hands and was the first person to release a totally digital performance mix CD for the Renaissance label in 2004, entitled 'ALiVE'.

Since then there's been a flood of totally digital mixes released into the market leaving Sasha in no doubt as to the future of house music.

I was looking for what was next, he explained to LA City Beat. I think I got to the point where I'd achieved a lot of things and a lot of career goals and I was thinking: 'What's next?' I feel a self-imposed pressure to keep things fresh for myself, but there's also a pressure from the crowds who want to see you doing stuff that's exciting. As long as you keep doing that, you've got a career.

This insatiable thirst to keep moving forward with technology has maintained his presence in the top five of most DJ polls conducted throughout his career and he's not about to stop just yet.

The accessibility has taken some of the mystery away from DJing, he continued. I used to come to America and play for people. There was no way they could get those records, and so there was a uniqueness to my sound.

Now it's everywhere, but that pushes it to another level. The technology will move things forward and enable you to give unique performances every time you play. A set of Technics turntables and a mixer is not enough now. It's time to move on.

Global Underground had already approached Sasha a year earlier with a view to a new mix CD to add to their escalating series of compilations that consistently live up to the slogan 'travelling the world with the speed of sound'.

His views on a compilation CD had taken on a different slant, as he became familiar with the new technology available to him, in particular a program called Ableton Live. This was a sampling and sequencing program that would allow the user to add a live element to a DJ set, throwing snippets and edits of tracks into a mix, in time and on beat, with the click of a mouse.

> *I actually signed up with Global Underground to do a normal mix compilation, Sasha told Ibiza Voice. But I wasn't getting enough out of it. And, after all the work I did on my own album, to do a normal mix album felt like a step backwards. But with this, I was able to combine my DJ and production work in one project seamlessly.*

The name for the compilation was decided as 'Involver' and would include just 10 tracks as opposed to the usual double CD format. Nonetheless each track was effectively a unique remix by Sasha's own fair hand, each one re-edited to blend seamlessly into each other using the new capabilities that Ableton Live offered.

The inspiration behind the project developed whilst he was on a boat as opposed to the regular process in a studio.

> *The way this came about was when we were at a boat party in Miami at the Winter Music Conference for a preview of the release of 'Involver'. Everyone was asking me for samples of the songs on 'Involver'. I knew how the tracks were supposed to sound finished but I had them in parts, not really finished versions. I went ahead and played five or six tracks in Ableton Live and I prolonged the tracks as much as I could and that's when a light bulb went off in my head.*

The concept behind a radical new way of DJing had been put in place with the ability to combine the skills of a DJ with the talents of a live artist. Sasha realised the possibilities with Ableton were endless, but nevertheless it took a few months road testing before he was completely satisfied with the final prototype as a DJ tool.

> It's amazing because it was a total pie in the sky dream that I had, but I was lucky enough to find the right people to do it. It's enabled me to find my groove once again.

Having now transferred his vast vinyl collection of more than 30,000 records to a database on his Apple Mac, he is now truly 100 per cent digital. DJing with a mouse and two laptops still lacks the coolness of touching and manipulating vinyl, but Sasha enthused about Ableton's abilities to LA City Beat.

> The great thing about Ableton is that everything on screen can be manipulated by MIDI, Musical Instrument Digital Interface. Everything that's on the screen you can assign a button, knob or fader to. You can basically customise it.

Unfortunately Ableton was built primarily for use in a studio environment so to take it into the DJ booth would require some modification. So Sasha immediately got to work on designing a customised controller to sit in between two laptops as a replacement for the industry standard mixer. The result was a robust looking piece of kit in brushed steel with rows of knobs, flashing lights and a cross fader than wouldn't look out of place in a cockpit. He nicknamed it the 'Maven'.

> I built it myself because there was really nothing on the market that you could use as an Ableton controller. I tried to stay as true to a normal DJ mixer as possible because that's what I know, he told Ibiza Voice.

> I've played with a couple of people that have been sceptical before the set. Once they've seen what I'm doing, they're like 'That's cool'. Whether they're going to switch over is another matter.

> I think it is going to have a big impact, but it isn't for everyone. It's enabled me to recreate that smokescreen which brings the magic into the experience. If that magic is revealed and we don't have that smokescreen, people lose interest simply because they are no longer surprised.

God is a DJ*

With his whole collection entirely at his disposal each time he plays, the possibilities are endless.

> *The Ableton is not really a new way of DJing, it's more like a new different option of a way of DJing and live remixing, a kind of a 'mashup' between the DJ and the live artist, he said. But in the end what comes out of the speakers is still a DJ set. There are so many things that I've always wanted to do with my DJ sets, but the technology was limited. With the Ableton Live there are a million things that I'm now able to do. It's completely re-energised me. It's like a live performance every night. It's the ultimate DJ experience.*

And that's what Sasha has always been about, pushing boundaries and finding new ways to excite both himself and his audiences as he expressed in full to Brent Meinema of 365Mag shortly before his latest compilation 'Involver" was released in 2004.

> *I'm never satisfied. In the last couple of years I've achieved some of the goals that I had set myself, such as attaining the top position in the DJ Mag poll and releasing my artist album Airdrawndagger. These are the things I thought about and worked towards. But as soon as you've achieved one thing, you have to keep pushing. I spent a month in the studio, playing around with records, I made a nice mix CD, but it didn't really grab me by the balls. It wasn't really exciting. So I started playing around with re-edits and remixes and then I thought: 'Why don't I remix every track?'*

> *So I started phoning everyone who's been so supportive. Underworld, Chemical Brothers, all these amazing people have been giving me the parts of their records, so I can completely rework them. So it's basically half a mix compilation and half an artist album, because I'm going to completely re-invent all the songs.*

> *First of all it has to be something that you can apply your sound to. I get sent so many tracks from people who want me to remix their work, and when it's a dance track it's hard for me to then re-interpret it and re-invent it. But when you hear a track that's*

from a different sound, perhaps a techno record that can be re-interpreted to break beat, then it gets interesting.

I want to create something that's going to blow up on the dance floor and also something that you can listen to at home. When you hear it on the dance floor you hear the simple elements, but when you listen to it at home you hear the full depth. I'm a DJ, so everything comes from the dance floor first. All my producer's standards come from what I have learned from being a DJ. That's why it's so important for me to still DJ while I'm producing

Even with the record Xpander, take the original version, I made a mix of it and I played it out and the last breakdown didn't work. So I went back into the studio and re-edited it and made it much stronger, so that last breakdown of Xpander is now a massive thing. So it's very important to me to be able to road test it, because when you're in the studio you get so close to something that sometimes you just can't step back and realise where things are at. When you put it out in a nightclub you know instantly if it works, or if it doesn't – it's a continuous process.

It's not like the old days when you had tape machines and you had to book a studio. If something doesn't work I put it on my laptop, so even on the plane to a gig I can re-edit the song, making the breakdown 16 bars longer or shorten it or whatever! That night I can put it onto a CD and can test it out. A lot of times I finish a record, but I'll make 4 or 5 different re-edits before I deliver the final mix to the record company.

The release of 'Involver' introduced the innovative concept of the Ableton to the attention of the masses, which Sasha describes as an evolution of *Airdrawndagger*.

This brought about not only a tour but also a bi-coastal residency incorporating his adopted hometown New York and Los Angeles at happening nightclubs Crobar and Avalon respectively. Each night sold out continuously over the six-month schedule, confirming Sasha's ever growing popularity in the States.

During this period of bedding in with the revolutionary new Maven controller and Ableton software he was able to stretch the capabilities of the new set up, playing up to six tracks simultaneously.

God is a DJ*

Blown away by such a positive reaction to the live gigs, the foundations for his new project were firmly afoot. Completed in a matter of days, 'Fundacion' would be the second release on the Global Underground label within the year, attesting to the forward strides made by Sasha since starting his new DJ revolution.

> 'Involver' was my experiment with Ableton, my remix project. It really pushed the capabilities of Ableton in the studio. Sasha told Inspired PR. 'Fundacion' captures what I can now do with Ableton in a live capacity, this is my mix album.

The CD totally captured the sound of his current hometown gigs at Crobar in New York whilst the cover art was shot within a block of his house, giving that personal feel to the album.

This has in turn given rise to a series of 'Fundacion' mix albums based in cities around the world with LA to be used as the next instalment following his monthly achievements at Avalon.

The 'Fundacion' tour expanded to Ibiza for the summer where he joined forces with Steve Lawler for an irresistible back-to-back set on the last Thursday of each month at Steve's new 'VIVA' night on the legendary Space terrace. Following an extensive refurbishment including a proper roof, it was for the first time to be open until 6am for what promised to be an unforgettable summer.

The final part of the Fundacion tour will be at the spectacular Womb nightclub in Tokyo later in the year for four weeks of digital mayhem and madness. He told Clare Woodcock from Get Involved exactly why he had chosen to use Womb.

> I'm going out there for a month and hosting Fundacion at Womb, which is my favourite club out there. There's a couple of other clubs in Tokyo that are great, such as Yellow, which is a smaller place and it's amazing. But I chose Womb because I love it. The guys that designed Womb used to live in New York when Twilo was on there and they were insistent on creating that kind of club in Tokyo. So they actually got the Twilo sound system and had it built at Womb. It's got an amazing energy in that club.

> I've only started playing Japan in the last two or three years and my name went from zero to 100 out there very quickly through a couple of strong gigs at Womb, so I'm really looking forward to actually hosting it for a month. Jeff Mills does that once a year in

21 Cooling down: Sasha takes a minute, Jacksonville, Florida, USA, 1999. (*Courtesy of Angela Collins*)

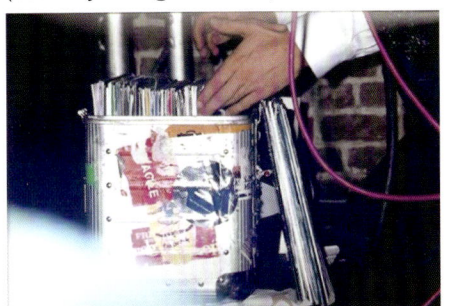

22 The box of magic: Sasha at work in Jacksonville, 1999. (*Courtesy of Angela Collins*)

23 The main event: Sasha enthrals another main room, this time at Space, Ibiza, 1999.

24 Turning heads: Live at Café Mambo, Ibiza, Summer 2002.

25 Taking a minute: Tanned and relaxed while launching the awesome *Global Underground* mix at Café Mambo.

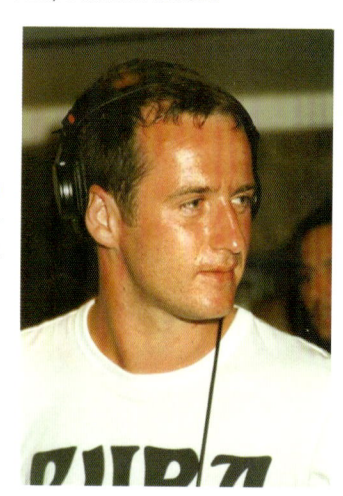

26 Night games: The twilight hours at Twilo, New York, 2005.

27 Rising to the top: Sasha at Cream, Liverpool, 2002.

28 Vital equipment: If these headphones could only talk, what a story they would tell – Sankeys, Manchester, 2003.

29 When vinyl ruled the world: Another legendary set at Tribal Sessions, Sankeys, Manchester, 2003.

30 Eastern promise: Sasha playing to the masses live in Bucharest, 2005. (*Courtesy of Sal Badalucco*)

sasha 2005 technical rider.

Sasha to supply:
1x Maven Controller
1x iMac G5
1x Wireless Keyboard
1x Wireless Mouse
1x Hard Drive Recorder

Promoter to supply:
1x Small Table for CD
(in front of left monitor)
2x Pioneer CDJ-1000s
1x Allen & Heath V6 Mixer
(sunk into table)
1x Electric Fan
2x Dimmable Lights
1x Large Table 4x8ft (folding)
covered in acoustical foam
(if the set-up is not in the booth)

Additional Notes:
Sasha needs control of the 2x monitor speakers graphic EQs and lighting of the dj booth

The Maven Controller MUST be plugged into Channel 6 on the Allen & Heath V6 Mixer.

If a V6 is unavailable please install an Allen Xone 62, Xone 92 or Rane rotary with seperate eq's.
In that order of preference

MONITOR with Sub (LEFT)
MONITOR with Sub (RIGHT)

STEREO MONITORS MUST CREATE AUDIO SWEET SPOT
RAISED TO WAIST HEIGHT, AND AT 180 DEGREES TO EACH OTHER

31 The magician reveals his tricks: Sasha's technical rider, 2005.

32 Sun kissed: Sasha is that good, he can even get the sun to set with the flick of a switch – Miami Boat Party, March 2006. (*Courtesy of Jason Warth*)

33 Happy Days: When Sasha smiles, so does Shanghai. A sign he has gone truly global, 2005.

34 I love my job: Sasha battles on at Le Souk in New York despite distractions, 2006. (*Courtesy of Jason Warth*)

35 Milking the crowd: . . . and they bloody love it. Sasha & Digweed, April 2008. (*Courtesy of Jason Warth*)

36 Remember this? Sasha at Amnesia, Ibiza, August 2007.

37 Brewing up a storm: Sasha at The Warehouse Project, December 2007.

38 Prime pairing: Sasha and John Digweed took America to the next level with their landmark Spring tour, 2007.

39 A dream come true: The beautiful Paula Pedroza with her idol talking all things house, 2010.

40 In the zone: Live in the mix at the Haçienda 25th anniversary at Urbis, Manchester, July 2007. (*Courtesy of Alex Kirkley*)

41 Me and him: The author with Sasha at Urbis, Manchester, during a July 2007 celebration night marking 25 years since the legendary Haçienda opened.

the summertime and it really works. I'll probably do a couple of nights on my own and a couple where I invite guests to play with me, we haven't quite worked it out yet.

It's great to do a big long set on my own, but then there's some DJs that I love playing with and I get a real energy from playing back-to-back with them and a different set comes out of me. Playing with other DJs really pushes you in different directions. I played with Josh Wink recently at Crobar and he ended up making me play like a techno DJ, it was amazing. It was so much fun I was grabbing bits of his set, he was looping bits from mine, it was constant loops and filters – just this wall of sound and everyone was saying 'Fucking hell, it sounds so different'. He kept on pushing me to play in a different way. It wasn't like I was playing whole tracks. I was grabbing bits of tracks and looping them. It was really exciting. And then playing with someone like Lee Burridge at the Exit Festival in Serbia recently – you've got a whole different sound, really funky and twisted sound. It just keeps you fresh playing with other DJs. You can spend so much time on the road on your own, you can get caught up in your own bubble. It's good to keep mixing things up.

In between such global residencies, the remainder of Sasha's time has been spent flying around Europe spreading the Fundacion word to sell-out crowds eager to hear what the rest of the world had already sampled.

London's Fabric was one venue lucky enough to be privileged to get a leg of the UK tour. Unable to make that date, I had my fingers crossed for Sankeys Soap to get the northern vote. However, it was Liverpool and a relatively new night that would get the nod. 'Circus' at the Masque nightclub had become THE night to be at in Liverpool, now that Cream had relinquished its grip. It's situated not far from the regenerated Albert Dock area of Liverpool that is now thriving with a host of new contemporary bars and restaurants.

The idea started out as a mere hobby for the local DJ Yousef, who was described as being more popular than Michael Owen during his short lived residency at Cream. The original plan was to showcase a monthly night at Cream, which had become his spiritual home during his late teens. Unfortunately, due to the demise and subsequent

God is a DJ*

closure of the one-time super club, Yousef was forced to seek alternative accommodation for his brainchild.

Fortunately close friend Rich McGinnis, a well-liked promoter around Liverpool, was also looking for a new venue for his own project 'Chibuku Shake Shake', which had outgrown its original venue. Together they salvaged a disused theatre in the summer of 2002 and transformed it into what is now an established upfront house club at the forefront of the UK scene.

The success culminated in the prestigious Radio 1 House Rules award for Club of the Year for 2005, and Yousef was delighted to achieve such recognition for his efforts.

The concept of Circus is simple – serious house music and a fun time. I'm booking DJs and acts that have and will inspire me, he said.

I can't really believe we have been doing this for three years. And winning 'House Rules Club of the Year' was unbelievable too. We work hard to put on a great party each month and we always try to make it clear to each DJ it's not just about them but rather the vibe of the club and the people – we are all part of it. My hobby is now one of the UK's best nights without question.

All things considered, it was the obvious choice for the North West leg of the Fundacion tour and being only 25 miles from home, it was ideal for me to check out what all the fuss was about.

Once the date had been confirmed, I contacted the ever-obliging Claire at Sasha's DJ agency Excession to confirm my guest list request for Gareth, Richard and myself, and as ever she obliged with the click of a mouse and an email.

Although as I mentioned I only live 25 miles from Liverpool, it's still an expensive taxi unless someone volunteers to drive. On any given Sasha night the raised hands for drivers are rarer than rocking horse shit as each of us would much rather sink some, or a lot, of Budweisers than spend half the night pissing diet coke.

And so the decision to stay over at a hotel was made without much fuss in the knowledge that the new budget Formule 1 chain is the ideal choice for any clubbing nights at a city centre near you. A mere £27 for a room that sleeps three in the heart of the Albert Dock area with a self-cleaning communal shower and toilet facility for me translates into clubbers' utopia, seeing as you only spend five hours in the thing. The communal bathroom proves to be just an excuse to meet people, weird, wonderful and downright strange, seeing as the queue in the corridor at 5am is as long as a fortnight. That's two weeks where I come from!

The night in question had arrived along with the celebrated British summer. From the moment we got in the car it never stopped raining. Not ones to be put off by a few inches of torrential rain, we checked into our salubrious dwelling for the night then jumped in someone else's taxi that had fortuitously arrived at the door upon our exit.

Seel Street in the centre of town has numerous bars to choose from with Bar Fly, which regularly hosts pre-club parties for various nights, being our preferred destination.

I tend to judge the quality of a bar not on the drinks served but the clientele and soundtrack. And on entering the contemporary, industrial-looking bar I was assured we were in the right place judging from the vast array of quality footwear on show from the masses already enjoying their escape from the rain. Being a man of as many pairs of footwear as I have T-shirts I hold my own opinion in high regard. Adidas and Puma held the majority vote with the exclusive T-3 and 96 Hours ranges at the fore, although a few other unique pairs caught my eye whilst I waited patiently for Gareth to return from the bar with the first round.

The music pumping out of the generous PA system was quite cool, laid back house that complemented its surroundings. Loud enough to hear but low enough to chat whilst the bass was enough to make your feet shuffle.

After a few rounds and a couple of tequilas thrown in to get the party started, we decided to venture outside towards the club. The rain had not relented and so refuge was sought half way there in another bar, in order to ensure at least our socks were still dry. By this time, it was 11pm and last orders had been called promptly, leaving us with no option but to down our drinks and hotfoot it to the club for our first experience of the Masque.

My first observation on arrival at the entrance was one of confusion. A Sasha night and no huge queue of people? This was a first for all three of us as we cautiously entered what resembled the pub we had been in previously.

God is a DJ*

Inside, the confusion continued as only a small gathering of people were dancing to some sleazy house music coming from the far side of what appeared to be a pub. We looked at each other and questioned whether we had got the right venue or had Sasha cancelled without our knowing? The fact that no one had yet asked for our tickets or names on the guest list was even stranger.

As we ventured further into the venue, I spotted the familiar figures of the most animated and watchable DJs I've ever seen, Tim Sheridan of Dope Smugglaz fame with his DJ partner Smokin Jo behind the decks set up in the far reaches of the room. A large vinyl banner highlighting their own night, 'NastyDirtySexMusic', was draped behind them under a throbbing, deep red spotlight, adding a devious undercurrent to the ambience of the room. Their night had been a huge success over the past two years with a solid reputation built at various venues in Ibiza. I had not seen the flyer for the night so presumed they were playing the warm up set, although it was pretty full on for a warm up.

Still there remained no sign of Sasha or the usual hordes that ensue on his arrival. By chance, we saw two sweat-laden clubbers emerge from a doorway concealed in the blackness of the décor, drinking profusely from water bottles.

Recognising that there was another room to investigate, the three of us immediately headed for the doorway in the far corner of the club that emitted the flashing beam of a strobe light, only to be stopped by the arm of a member of security blocking our passage.

We'd found Sasha, only to be told, much to our dismay, that the room was already full to capacity. We explained our names would be on the list, at which point he led us to the all-too-familiar clipboard girl to confirm our status. Having had our names checked off, we hastily made our way downstairs, following the hypnotic, sonorous sounds coming from below.

A thick, heavy, black curtain covered the entrance to the main room and on levering it aside, we unveiled a whole other world. It was like lighting the blue touch paper. The atmosphere was electrifying and the place was absolutely rammed.

Now this was what I call a typical Sasha night. The PA system encapsulated the room with everyone moving in unison to the beats. I somehow felt like I had missed out on the first part of the night, as I wasn't yet on the same level as everyone else around me.

As we ventured into the foray, I noted the DJ booth was immediately to my right on a raised platform which I presumed would have been the stage in this former theatre. Surrounding the booth on all three sides were ardent clubbers locked into the musical excursion that Sasha was about to take them on.

The main hub of the dance floor was quite unique with terracing as if you were in a football stadium. The format worked beautifully though as even those at the farthest point from the booth were elevated enough to enable them to see and feel the night progressing.

Having managed to lever our way through the crowd directly in front of the booth, the three of us got involved in the commotion on the dance floor, carving out our own little niche so as to be able to feel each track evolve.

Sasha stood, head bowed, fixed into his groove, lit only by the lights radiating from the large screens of the laptops on either side of him. It was strange not to see him ducking down out of sight momentarily behind the decks while he foraged for the next slab of vinyl from his box, but his digital set up now means everything is within reach of his fingertips.

It wasn't long before I caught sight of Sparrow leaping about behind Sasha, who appeared almost static in comparison. As soon as he caught my attention, he gestured for the three of us to join him behind the decks for a reunion of sorts, seeing as we'd not seen each other for at least six months.

It took a few minutes to escape our much lauded vantage point near the front of the dance floor, which we had edged our way to seemingly unnoticed. Sparrow was holding the rear door to the booth open when we finally snaked our way through. As DJ booths go, this one was quite spacious in comparison with others where there's little room for records let alone guests, and it had a separate section where Sasha was performing.

The first thing to catch my eye was that both laptops were sat on top of the Technics turntables. That was something of a statement. This was DJing for the 21st century. For 25 years, Technics turntables were the industry benchmark for quality, and had more than lived up to their reputation, but now it was time to step aside as they were now clearly surplus to requirements.

The new Maven midi controller sat proudly between the two large screen laptops in all its polished glory. Each track that comes in is

God is a DJ*

manipulated and rearranged using mainly two channels on the Maven, with the custom cross fader taking a hammering in the process. The crowd appeared to be at the mercy of this new tool as Sasha looped and fused elements from different tracks to make his performance live in every sense of the word.

As the Guerillaz' *Feel Good Inc* track cut in over a rolling kick drum, the crowd responded to its familiarity, and with a flick of the Maven, in came Sasha's very own *Wavy Gravy* track in perfect time. The crowd reacted instantaneously with cheers and screams as the tempo increased once again.

Sasha's beaming smile made it obvious for all as to how thrilled he was to see his new set up working harmoniously with the masses, and his arms punched the air in unison with the impassioned crowd in front. Yousef was stood next to me, taking in the new heights that his own creation had reached and seeing nothing but smiling faces surrounding him.

Many of Sasha's old friends from the North had now occupied the DJ booth with quite a few familiar faces that I'd not seen in a while, in particular John Sutton of Evolution fame who has frequently worked with Sasha throughout his career, remixing and producing on various projects.

Whilst Richard and I went mad to the next track beating in, Gareth somehow managed to get himself lost on his return from the bar as his text message "Where have you gone?" verified. As we hadn't moved from where he left us, I presumed he'd had another bout of amnesia, as this occurrence was becoming increasingly frequent on nights out.

Last summer on a night in the opulent yet sprawling Pacha nightclub in Ibiza, he managed to lose both of us not once but three times for what must have been an hour at a time over the course of the night.

A vodka induced text message similar to the one I had just received quickly followed, conversely reading "MEER WER WU," which I deduced as "Where are you?" This was after three equally inebriated phone calls during which we tried to guide him back to the main room, which led to one journey down a fire exit and another into the kitchens where a money counting scene from the film 'Casino' was apparently taking place. We headed back out onto the dance floor; unable to detect him from our prime spot in the booth, but no sooner had we returned to our previous spot at the front of the dance floor than Gareth duly arrived, muttering something about Robert De Niro!

Back to Masque, and now regrouped, we instantly got back into the flow of things with Sasha becoming visibly more animated as the night progressed towards its climax. The last hour was approaching and I realised that if we weren't able to be readmitted to the DJ booth, Sasha would be whisked off back to his hotel at the end of the night without me being able to pass the time of day with him, let alone have a chat.

Sparrow once again obliged with the door duties to enable the three of us to regain our positions right next to the large monitor speaker. From there you could hear every drum kick, synth noise, echo and effect that his Ableton set up could throw out.

I knew it was the ideal spot from the moment Sasha dropped Thomas Newman's *Drive Away* track which roared through the PA system with the galvanising undercurrent of Ewan Pearson's mighty dub version of Moby's *Raining Again* hammering out stabs of thunder that spewed out onto the dance floor.

The reverent crowd erupted with delight, their thirst for one more track to take them to that 'higher state of consciousness' apparent on their faces. Sasha, visibly willing the crowd to demand another piece of magic, used his innate ability to produce another unforgettable end-of-night moment.

The grinding, retro-futuristic synths of The Killers' *Mr Brightside* remix came to the fore as the previous tracks simmered in the background. The surging bassline built up to an incredible tempo, charging the whole room so that when the chorus broke in sync with the lights and strobes that flash in time with the racing heartbeats that surround the DJ booth, level '11' was reached on the volume.

That's as good as it gets, but sadly it was the last record. The main lights switched on to reveal hundreds of perspiring faces all beaming with the same glow of another fantastic night to add to the memory bank.

I squeezed past the monitor to give Sasha a customary hug and handshake. We passed the usual pleasantries and a quick chat about his pending marriage to Zoië. I'm lucky to be able to recall most of my nights in his company but what kind of memory would be needed to remember all the unforgettable Sasha nights?

Epilogue

The Warehouse Project
Manchester, 2006–2010

"The Sasha myth is a potent one, not based purely on media hype or good looks, more on his spellbinding ability to catch the mood of the crowd and weave it into a hypnotic maelstrom. When Sasha finishes one of his sets, people are liable to get emotional. You could call it trance. I call it magic!"

Dom Phillips

HALFWAY through a decade is usually a time for reflection on what has gone before and what is about to happen. Some tread with trepidation while others pursue the unknown with fervour and an eagerness to succeed.

The year 2006 was quite a landmark in terms of the changing way we looked at things and a realisation of how fast life had become in such a throwaway culture. For instance, the iPod generation were now downloading millions of tracks each day and the CD single was becoming surplus to requirements for those who already demanded instant access to their favourite genre.

With such soaring demands for that instant hit of music and the necessity to have it yesterday, it was with a heavy heart that the Official UK Charts Company decided there was a need to organise an official UK Download Chart.

In early January 2005, the week before the 1,000th number one single topped the UK Singles Chart, legal downloads overtook physical sales for the first time in UK chart history, and this has been the case ever since. CD sales throughout early 2005 were very poor and all-time records for lowest sales were being constantly set.

Therefore, on 17th April 2005, for the first time the official UK Singles Chart incorporated legal downloads as well as physical sales. For all you statisticians out there, the first official Number One track on the download chart was The Pixies' *Bam Thwok* . . . What a classic!

Epilogue

Total accessibility had now become imperative to all and sundry with virtually everyone over the age of nine seemingly communicating via a mobile phone or a social networking site. Television now gave us a choice of more than 140 channels, letting us watch pretty much what we wanted whenever we liked.

The summer of 2006 witnessed one of the most watched events in television history with an estimated 26.29 billion viewers tuning in to the World Cup Final tournament in Germany, the final attracting an estimated audience of 715.1 million people.

House price inflation had jumped into double digits for the first time in nearly two years with the housing market kicking off 2007 in rude health. The average house price had increased by £45 every day during 2006. These further rises of house prices had surprised many analysts who concluded that the market looked dangerously stretched in relation to historical averages, increasing the possibility of a housing market crash, especially with unemployment continuing to rise. How right they were.

But while all major events in a year seemed to look forward without fearing the past, as 2006 came to a close, clubland would be taken back kicking and screaming 20 years by the people who had resurrected the once derelict Sankeys Soap into one of the major players not only in Manchester but throughout the UK.

Sacha Lord-Marchionne and his new team of directors, Sam Kandel, Kirsty Smith and Richard McGinnis, launched the audacious 'Warehouse Project'.

The location, described as 'one of Manchester's most iconic landmarks in the heart of the city centre' was The Old Brewery, on the site of the former Boddingtons Brewery with its famous chimney protruding out over the nearby and relatively new Manchester Evening News Arena.

Boddingtons was dubbed 'the cream of Manchester' for many years during their advertising campaigns, and it would have been easy to reuse this slogan. However, there was another Cream not too far down the road in Liverpool, so they wisely changed their tagline to 'For 12 weeks This City is Ours' and for that period from October onwards each year since 2006, Manchester has become a different beast.

Secrecy over such a bold and courageous venture was of the upmost importance to ensure its launch was not jeopardised in any way, and so cloak and dagger meetings were held around the country

God is a DJ*

with some of the most seminal people in dance music from DJs to agents to artists.

The opening night on Thursday, 5th October 2006, featured the legendary Public Enemy. However, this was far from a one-off media stunt as acts of equal stature streamed through the doors and onto to the stage to entertain and engross the thousands who begged, pleaded and bid for tickets to the most sought after events Manchester has staged since those snaking queues at the Haçienda on any given Saturday night during its pomp in 89/90.

Virtually every genre of dance music has been covered since the opening night and no matter what type of night has been offered, there has been a seemingly guaranteed sell out which is some feat considering the size of the venue.

Kirsty spoke to Rachel Esson of *Night* magazine in 2008 and explained some of the complexities of hosting such a huge event.

> *It was a complete beast, she said, referring to the cavernous old brewery. It was massive and we had well over 100,000 people through the doors. We arrived with a bit of a storm, which was good, and I think the challenge is to develop it. Each year we want to keep it as exciting as when people first heard about The Warehouse Project. We had a few issues at Boddingtons due to sound leaks and we had some complaints from the nearby Strangeways Prison. Boddingtons wasn't designed for a rave down, it was designed to make beer. The roof is made of tin and the cost of insulating that place was not viable.*

The list of DJs and bands that have appeared reads like a who's who of today's dance music industry, to a point where if you named the top 20 DJs and live acts in the world, chances are they have played there.

Obviously there was one night in particular I noted down in my diary as the one not to miss as soon as the line-ups are announced, and Sasha appearing on the e-flyer also guaranteed a flurry of interest on the Facebook and Twitter sites.

Whilst Sacha and Kirsty worked tirelessly to ensure the biggest names in dance music, past and present, were committed to performing at this monumental event, both Sam and Richard McGinnis were tasked with securing the services of Sasha. The team were well aware that securing his talent would send a huge message out to punters and promoters alike that the Warehouse Project was destined to be the real deal.

Sam and Richard had crossed paths on numerous occasions during their clubbing careers as promoters and were eager to join forces to ensure they obtained maximum exposure for the Warehouse Project. Sam became more prominent in the booking of DJs during his inauguration to clubland at Sankeys whilst Rich cut his teeth down the road at Manchester's antithesis Liverpool.

I only recently met Rich, but it soon became apparent that we had spent years in the same room in clubs throughout the world. It was comforting to know that Rich was told who I was by none other than the pied piper of dance music Pete Tong. He had spotted me at the front of the crowd when hosting the monumental 500th Essential Selection night at the Masque in Liverpool and asked Pete who I was as he'd seen me dozens of times before at various events up and down the country.

Hailing originally from Belfast, Rich had come over to Liverpool in 1995 at a time when Cream were fast becoming a superclub, and surrounded himself with like-minded people who like myself, were enchanted by the dance scene. I soon realised that Rich is a charming man who makes things happen and consequently good things happen to him.

Having witnessed the rise of Cream in his newly adopted home town he decided to make his own way in clubland by starting up his own night called 'Chibuku Shake Shake', the name being taken from a weird South African beverage that is known to locals as the beer of good cheer.

Rich's good fortune coincided with the surprise closing of Cream in October 2002. The launch of Chibuku had suddenly been handed another potential 3,000 redundant clubbers eager to get their weekly house fix. This situation was then suddenly compounded when only weeks later the only other major club night in Liverpool, Garlands, was also forced to close after a fire gutted the building.

This left Rich with a new night at a new venue along with the problem of how to house the city's clubbing fraternity. Something he managed with aplomb and would prove to be a major player in clubland in the North West of England.

Both Rich and Sam came into constant contact with each other, many times sharing the cost of flights for some international DJs so

God is a DJ*

they could play Sankeys one night and Chibuku the next. They also had another thing in common in that they both recognised the significant effect that booking Sasha had on their respective nights.

The Warehouse team had plotted and arranged to ensure Sasha would play at one of the opening weekends and so Rich and Sam were tasked with meeting his UK management team at his own Excession DJ agency in London. Sasha's company had assembled an impressive line-up of DJs to their roster including James Zabiela, Steve Lawler and Sander Kleinenberg, all of whom would add considerable weight to the Warehouse line ups.

Good relationships between parties had already been established and so it was just a matter of convincing Excession executive Tara Morgan that The Warehouse Project would become the biggest music event in Manchester's prestigious history. Whatever was said in the meeting was obviously enough to persuade Tara that bringing Sasha to the event would benefit both parties immensely. A good decision I think.

Friday, 8th December 2006, was officially freezing in Manchester. As confirmed by the dashboard thermometer in our designated driver Jen Harvey's now classic Peugeot 307 circa '95 that read a big fat zero.

But the thought of standing in a huge empty warehouse drinking cold lager was soon put to the back of my mind by the warming sight of a huge queue snaking around the old Boddingtons brewery, safe in the knowledge that Sasha was headlining. I would no doubt be surrounded by like-minded clubbers eager to soak up the atmosphere and exchange body heat, so to speak. I also had a good winter coat and scarf to hand as I am now at that age where a coat is staple attire unless I can actually see the sun.

The vast concrete space that once housed a thriving brewery had many empty disused office and factory units strewn around, with huge metal gates fencing off some areas with safety in mind of course.

I watched people pointing and chatting excitedly as the mini-crowds converged on what was basically a massive warehouse with its regulation huge warehouse door that reached maybe 30 feet high. From behind this came a throb of bass spewing out into the courtyard area.

On the opposite side was an impressive array of green rectangular boxes, so many being present that the end of this row of boxes was not even in sight. Thankfully these weren't mere decoration but the

Epilogue

quintessential portable toilets that would be put through their paces by the end of the night.

We had arrived around the witching hour to hear Sasha's long time friend and studio partner Charlie May, under his customary guise of Spooky, warming the crowd nicely with a deep house vibe that had a somewhat retro feel to it.

The front of the vast stage to the right of us was beginning to swell and a clearly visible arc had formed around the middle of the stage where the decks stood. The decks were subtly lit with a blue downlight but were elevated high enough above everyone's eyeline to ensure maximum visibility. On each side of the stage were huge 30-feet visual screens projecting warping images that played with your mind in time with the music.

To the left at the rear of the 'club' was the main bar that was probably the length of a football pitch and armed with staff all adorned with black Warehouse Project T-shirts with 'Bar Staff' emblazoned in white on the back. These became so sought after, that people were later bidding upwards of £50 each for them on eBay. Needless to say, there is now a full merchandising arm to this moneymaking entertainment machine. It would not be like the Warehouse Project's kingpin Sacha to miss an opportunity like that.

To me, the ease of getting served at the bar is essential to a good vibe in the place and wherever Sacha and his team has run events, this small but important detail has always been taken care of. If people have to wait 20 minutes to get a drink, you've gotta work twice as hard to put the smile back on their face. Promoters take note.

From memory, I recall Sasha was due to play around 1am. I had sent him a text to say I would try and meet up at the new five star Lowry Hotel where he was staying and which was only two minutes from the venue, but we were both too pushed for time beforehand. Nonetheless I was eager to see him again prior to him going on stage in front of a now revved up 2,000 or so clubbers.

With our luminous backstage wristbands, courtesy of Kirsty Smith who welcomed us at the entrance and has always looked after myself and friends down the years, we headed for the unknown in the form of the VIP area.

A robust gentleman of some size and stature was guarding a certain section of iron railing next to the stage as if it had the Crown Jewels attached to it. Of course this was where access was gained and he let

God is a DJ*

us through without a fuss. No sooner had we cleared the stage area when we bumped into resident WHP director Sam Kandel who knew exactly where we wanted to head to.

The VIP area was basically a portable cabin on top of a storage unit. However, once inside you felt like you were in, well, a portable cabin on top of a storage unit, but with a Boddingtons bar, a dartboard and some emergency seating around the outskirts.

Yet I wasn't complaining as the drinks were free and the company great as I, Warby and Jenny held court with a few familiar faces from Sankeys days, such as John from Evolution and resident DJ Krysko and his girlfriend. As always the banter was great, the hot topic of the moment being how such an exciting new venue regaled the days of the original illegal warehouse raves that only a few of us could talk about first hand.

Sasha was still to appear and so we made our way to the back of the stage where, lo and behold, the 'man-like' turned up right on cue with a jam-packed sleeve of CDs in one hand and a laptop in the other. Admittedly, it was a freezing December night, but I almost didn't recognise him in a grey Bob Marley-style rasta hat. I suppose if it was good enough for Bob then fair enough. Sasha is also cool enough to pull that sort of hat off, the bastard.

He was really upbeat about his set, talking excitedly about some of his own reworked tracks that he was anxious to get a reaction on. I said I'd let him know my constructive thoughts, to which he smiled knowing I'm sometimes too honest.

As Sasha took to the stage, we went to jostle for a position near the front. Warby was always particularly good at gaining good vantage points so we let him take the lead. Budweisers in hand, we weaved and squeezed behind quite a number who were clinging to the front safety barriers, unwilling to give up their sought after front row spot for love nor money.

As he took to the decks, the temperature in the room has risen considerably to the point where I had removed my scarf. His first record brought a huge cheer to which he acknowledged with the raising of a hand. Even though Sasha would never acknowledge the fact that he was considered one of the best DJs in the world, I bet 90 per cent of the crowd that night would have given him their vote such was their devotion to their hero.

Epilogue

His set was typically upfront with many tracks brand new to the listening audience.

In the first few weeks, prior to Sasha's appearance, the sound in the Boddingtons warehouse was far from audiophile quality to say the least as the huge dampers that hung from the ceiling over the bar area struggled to cope with the barrage of noise from the vast PA system. From certain points in the room, you could hear the echo coming back with a slight delay that would be very annoying if you stood in that same spot throughout. However from near the front it was virtually unnoticeable.

Sasha had spoken to John Digweed, who had played the previous week, about this issue and expressed his concerns to the team as he was conscious of the impact his set would have not only on the public but also his peers and future promoters.

He spoke to Rich McGinnis extensively about how he thought the sound could be improved with a little tweaking of the arrangement of the speakers and offered to send his trusted sound engineer down prior to the gig to ensure maximum effect from the set up. The result from a few minor changes to speaker arrangements, tweeters and sub-woofers was a remarkable improvement on the original set up. This just goes to show what a perfectionist Sasha is and how much he cares for his trade.

The opening bars of Sasha's own club remix of The Chemical Brothers' *Out of Control* with its trademark ferocious beats came flooding through as the crowd stepped up a gear and Sasha became visibly more animated. It went down a storm as the night picked up pace but it was some of the newer tracks that caused more of a commotion.

Cubic's *Superstylin* was one of those surprise tracks that builds the energy with a rolling bass but its Italo Piano breakdown got the crowd's deserved attention. Another throwback to early Nineties house in the guise of Kosmas Epsolon's *Lovesong*, with its stabs of acid and 4 to 4 beat gave a real warehouse feel and the crowd responded instantly. This was one of many promos Sasha played that night but it was more than a year later that I managed to find the name of this acid monster.

Easier to track down was Laurent Garnier's *Crispy Bacon* with marauding techno beats and minimal synth twitters that eventually led into the crowd favourite, Sasha's own *Expander*, which guaranteed a

God is a DJ*

reaction no matter what anyone's issue with the sound system was. This track would sound great listened to through two cups and piece of string.

During 2006, Sasha's usual global exploits had culminated in another ground-breaking moment in the history of dance music.

Prior to one of his sets at his residency at the legendary Avalon Hollywood nightclub in the downtown glitz of Los Angeles, he had been approached by Instant Live, an on-site concert recording and distribution company to produce a completely live mix. The result came from that night, his set starting around 1.20am and enveloped the packed 1,400-capacity room in a halcyon tide of swells towards an unknown destination leaving some in a temporary state of zero gravity before bringing them to resounding climax. Clubbers attending this landmark closing party for Sasha's latest 'Fundacion' album tour would then be able to purchase a live recording of the set straight after the gig and take home their DJ hero on a double CD.

Sasha told the Resident Advisor website:

This is an amazing advancement in the use of technology. It just blows me away and it is truly exciting that it's possible to do something like this. This culture, like it or not, was built on bootlegs and now downloads. Instant Live allows me to put my sets directly into the hands of the fans while supporting the music makers. With the artwork and packaging, it will be a great memento of the night. This music has always been about immediacy, it really is here and now.

Unfortunately, the set was strewn with technical difficulties leading Sasha to later say he would never do something like that again, being the perfectionist he is. However, he was yet again the first DJ to embrace the new and keep one step ahead of the old.

One critic wrote of his DJing that night:

His style is more akin to travel. It journeys, it road trips, it does some sightseeing. It doesn't just sit in a pounding club all night. It may take in something a bit more cinematic and epic, which could very well crescendo to a frantic chase scene before settling back down with a nice Martini and engaging conversation. It lives.

Epilogue

The following 12 months saw Sasha take in not only three mini tours of the USA, covering eight states, but also three huge gigs in Sydney for the Double Vinyl Penetration crew, both Montreal and Toronto in Canada, and also Ukraine, Estonia and Romania. These dates accompanied his regular forays to Ibiza, Barcelona, Dublin, London and of course Manchester.

The year 2007 proved to be quite a productive year not only in terms of air miles but also as he even found some spare time to launch his own record label, Emfire, in August 2007, concentrating on both digital and vinyl outputs.

Speaking to 365mag.com he announced his intentions for the label.

It's been exciting getting back in the studio again after a hiatus, he said. I am looking forward to using this new imprint as a vehicle to release my own music as well as signing great forward thinking music from other producers.

The imprint will feature a strong, continuous graphic foundation. Running from release to release, a colour-coded, graded spectrum will marry to a numeric sequence. Insect, best known for their recent work with infamous UK graffiti artist Banksy, are handling the art direction. We want it to be simple, beautiful and collectible, particularly in terms of the vinyl.

Back to the Warehouse Project, and though they had only secured the Boddingtons venue for a short period, with such an exciting concept guaranteeing a successful first year, it was vital the team not only continued this phenomenon but improved on it. That was not such an easy task as they had to find a venue that could cope with a phenomenon so popular in excess of 1,800 people usually attended but also try to retain that warehouse ideology.

Directors Sacha, Sam, Rich and Kirsty needed to use all their clubbing experience, contacts and relationships to ensure the next venue would be everything the Old Brewery was and more. However, the choice of an underground car park in Piccadilly was to test not only themselves but the consuming public and also the design team.

Rachel Esson of Night magazine probed the team to find out exactly how difficult a task they had taken on. Local production company Ear to the Ground, who used to do production for the Haçienda, stepped

God is a DJ*

up to the plate and relished the prospect of taking on such a mammoth task.

Director John Drape explained the complexities of such an unusual concept ie levying 1,800 clubbers into an underground car park on a Friday and Saturday night, just hours after it closes, and making it look like the place never existed as a clubbers' venue by 7am on Monday morning. It was a logistical nightmare but Ear to the Ground took on the challenge of producing the events by assessing and preparing all aspects of safety, licensing, capacity, power and cabling, among other things.

> In terms of doing large nights and attracting big name DJs there hasn't been anything like it in the city since the Haçienda. The timescale we had on the Boddingtons Brewery made it hard, but once we had possession of it, it was ours for three months, whereas at Store Street, it's predominantly a car park so we've had to look at ways of putting in infrastructure that can stay in, but not be seen.

They made the car park 'rave-worthy' by supplying two generators, bars on wheels and discreet rigging points overhead in the brick work and into the rig on the stage, which takes up three parking bays and is blocked off overnight.

Rachel summed up the team's work in making the operation a smooth transition from car park to clubland, adding:

> Like the cars that pull up and park at Store Street midweek and get driven home at 5.30pm, the Warehouse Project rolled in and out of the venue like a surreal dream thanks to a slick operational process engineered by Kim and eased by the fact that 90 per cent of the 32 staff had been with the Project since the very beginning.

> The bars and sound proofing wall, which blocked off the new second room 'Bunker' at the back of the space this year, were literally rolled out of a cupboard for the evening's trade and pushed back again later on. The posters were taken down and the sound system locked away so that commuters would never imagine there had been crowds of sweaty clubbers dancing on their parking spot over the weekend.

Epilogue

Another constant came from the fact that the Warehouse Project team continued their relationship with sound production company Audile, whose own Rob Ashworth was tasked with ensuring any doubts about the sound quality were quickly put to bed.

The WHP did indeed used to be synonymous with sound issues. Noise spillage from the old Boddies venue meant that it had to run at an extremely low level, which was a huge problem, he said.

We were brought in when WHP moved to the current Store Street venue, where the sound issues have been overcome very successfully. In part this is due to the venue being an old air-raid shelter and the supporting structure to much of Piccadilly Station, so its walls are very thick! The position of the main dance floor in the second arch of the venue, and the orientation of the arches parallel to the road outside is also important. The way the system is configured in this space means it provides a great deal of isolation between the dance floor and the outside world.

It seemed all bases had been well and truly covered, though as the saying goes, the proof is in the eating. The popularity of this new venue increased year on year, as testified by the fact that gigs sold out literally within hours of being announced. The Chemical Brothers date in 2008 took just six hours to leave people with their only option but to start bidding on eBay for a ticket; such is the cult status that became attached to these so called club nights which now morphed into concert events thanks to the hype that surrounded them.

Sales increased by more than 100 per cent each year and I'm confident not many businesses worldwide could equal that. With production, marketing, staffing and sound all literally boxed off, it was just down to the team to add to their ever increasing DJ/artist roster of worldwide names as a fervent following stood by their laptops ready to book their place.

Moving to Store Street was a welcome change, said Kirsty. It gave us the ability to deliver the type of event we wanted to deliver production wise and the artists loved it. It was great to hear the artists say to their agents that one of the first dates for their diary was the Warehouse Project.

God is a DJ*

Sasha was no exception to this and took little persuading to come to such an exciting venue in what was for a long time his adopted home town, and his usual suite in the Lowry was duly booked.

His new Emfire label had been busy releasing his first brand new studio tracks since his 'Airdrawndagger' album in timely intervals as limited edition one-sided 12-inch singles. Starting with *Coma, Park it in the Shade*, whose title was taken from an order from one of the overzealous Ibizan police who told him where to park his car, *Who Killed Sparky* and *Mongoose*, all delivered in their own imitable way and transcended into the blueprint for the future of electronic house music while showcasing his versatility and sustained ability to devastate dance floors.

Sasha's own Emfire tracks featured heavily in his sets throughout the whole of 2007 and with audience reaction nothing short of emotional, I know how proud he was to get such awesome responses to the results of his 'day job'.

Friday, 14th December 2007, was to be Sasha's first taste of the new Shore Street venue and as expected he didn't disappoint such a diverse and cosmopolitan crowd. In the huge bar area to the side of the main room, we chatted to people from all over the country with groups from Newcastle, Leeds, Stoke and Jersey which only emphasised the huge following the Warehouse Project now fashioned. But when we came across a group from Portugal and two girls from Romania who were all on their travels but had specifically made sure that Manchester was a stop to be made at the end of the year to ensure they could make one of these cherished nights, we realised the global message being sent out by the Warehouse team.

By the time we got to the venue just before 1am, we were fortunate enough to catch the so-called warm up set from one the outstanding young DJ talents in the UK. James Zabiela, now having shaken off the shackles of being dubbed Sasha's protégé, was making a huge name for himself in his own right with festival bookings and compilation albums a plenty. His set demonstrated both his technical mastery of machines and deep understanding of music with sublime mixing blending all genres of house music that ensured the crowd were left wanting more.

Sasha appeared behind James as the latter still had a good 30 minutes left in his set but the crowd's anticipation now peaked as a surge for the last remaining spots in the main room soon developed.

Epilogue

Sasha was clearly out to impress and immediately took the crowd to the next level with his new studio works of art brought to the fore early on.

He saved his own *Park it in the Shade* for one of his closing records. This ocean-deep house monster breaks and beats and immerses you in swirling synths and stabs before bringing you back to the surface for another big gulp of air. But long before this crowd favourite sneaked in, the dance floor had reached sardine proportions with movement restricted to emergency toilet breaks and claustrophobia abounding. They had already been entranced by Davis and May's *Neotron*, a driving percussive track that builds with every beat and an eerie chime, as if stolen from an Ennio Morricone soundtrack. However my stand out track on this occasion was Swayzak's *Smile & Receive* which evoked more cinematic drama through a deep house vibe with haunting synth flooding through like a scene from a horror movie.

The Warehouse Project has since gone from strength to strength with Pete Tong, John Digweed, Deadmua5, David Guetta, Richie Hawtin and Paul Van Dyk just a few of the regular names ensuring their agents always book them for a repeat performance the following year.

Sasha was no exception and had not missed a year since the opening in 2006. Appearing with new Ibiza favourite Loco Dice in September 2008 to another sold out venue, he again delivered another masterclass, one of the highlights being the Zoo Brazil remix of Butch's *1,000 Lords*, a chugging, throbbing house monster alternating between the dark, demented sound of Europe and the cloud-parting optimism of his progressive past.

Fairmont's *I Need Medicine* demanded the crowd's attention with huge, bass filtered, echoing opening bars that physically passed through the body with a shudder, and Guy J's immense *Esperanza*, with its lingering atmospheric strings closed proceedings and another mesmeric performance.

As usual though, Sasha had a few tricks up his sleeve, even if that sleeve was on his favourite short sleeved black T-shirt, in the form of the classic Energy 52 track 'Café Del Mar' which surprised and delighted the masses as the lights went up in unison with everyone's arms. It was a photographer's dream shot that will no doubt stay long in the memory of those present, and the move to a new venue had been well and truly cemented in Manchester's already formidable

God is a DJ*

music history and would continue into the New Year. The only trouble now was being able to surpass what had gone before.

The following year, just when you thought things couldn't get any better, it was announced that on Friday, 18th December 12009, for the first time in almost a decade in Manchester, Sasha would be reunited with his partner-in-crime John Digweed. This followed on from a hugely successful spring tour of America the previous year after the annual music conference in Miami.

That was also the first time the pair had toured the since the Delta Heavy jaunt across America in 2002. Taking in 21 cities to maximise exposure across the country, the pair spoke extensively to DJ Ron Slomovicz of dancemusc.about.com shortly after finishing at the huge Coachella festival in California when they played in front of a crowd of almost 25,000.

DJ Ron has been writing for dancemusic.about.com for more than 10 years now, keeping the US informed of everything great and good in the world of house music.

Sasha told Ron in an interview prior to the tour:

We've been talking about doing it for a while. We'd done quite a few shows together in New York and LA, but we haven't toured together outside the US. It's just that we've both been doing a lot of work separately, touring separately and successfully, since Delta Heavy. We definitely took a break from each other. It wasn't like we fell out or anything, but we both had a lot of our own projects going on, so we both focused on our own things. Then last year, our calendars collided a lot more, and we ended up doing a lot of gigs together. It was a lot of fun so we talked about doing another American tour.

It's going to be fun. We're going to be back on the bus, doing four or five nights a week, stopping off in a lot of the smaller cities in-between the big cities. We're looking forward to it.

As for the production side of things, it needed some serious thought as to what kind of scale they would pitch it at.

It's not going to be as big and dramatic as the Delta Heavy tour. We made a conscious decision not to make it so grand. With the Delta Heavy tour, we had the arenas in mind. When we actually put it into a smaller venue, it was ridiculously large. To be

Epilogue

honest, most of the gigs on that Delta Heavy tour, where we had the most fun, were all the theatres, in the 1,500 to 3,000 size venues. They're the places we really enjoyed the most, where we felt our sound worked the best. So on this tour we've decided to concentrate on doing those kinds of venues, and to do some smaller clubs as well.

The production reflects that. It's a bit more minimal. We're using these really amazing new stealth LED screens, and building our set out of them. We've got this amazing visual arts company doing the programming for the screens and it looks pretty stunning. We did a gig up in Montréal together earlier on in the year, and these guys were doing the production for that. I saw what they'd done, and I was just absolutely blown away. So I asked them to do the whole tour with us and they were really into the idea. We've already had a gig with them and it just looks stunning. I think people are going to be impressed.

The crowds and critics alike were not let down.

Some of the sounds have definitely changed since the last time we were touring together, added Sasha.

I think the electronic music scene in general has changed a hell of a lot in the last six years, since we toured together. Definitely even in the last couple of years, with the Berlin movement on everyone's sound, I think it's become more minimal. But I still like to play records with melody and with warm sounds, and John still likes to play dark and dirty. I think that's why my music always complements his and vice versa.

In the last week of July 2009, tickets for the Sasha/Digweed event went on sale. By August there were only a few remaining, with many website forums and networking sites all touting for spare tickets for friends who were making the trip to Manchester specifically for this gig.

On 18th July 2009 I had become a dad to a beautiful little girl called Isla. As the actual date of the gig drew closer, the expectation grew and the night before I remember praying that she would sleep through for a full 12 hours to ensure my own slumber wasn't interrupted as I wanted to be on top form and fully rested for this special coming

God is a DJ*

together. Luckily Isla has been one of those babies everyone wants and like her mum, loves her sleep, so a restful night was had.

Waking up on Friday morning, I was full of beans and raring to go and to add to the anticipation of Sasha coming to town, I had been reading about his most recent gig in Melbourne when, playing the last gig of his mini-tour of Australia, he had unveiled the brand new pioneer CDJ2000 at the Billboard nightclub.

This new piece of kit had its official release a full 15 years after the genesis of Pioneer's first CDJ deck, which was championed as the 'dawn of a new species for the digital age' and will no doubt, as in the case of the Technics 1210 turntable, become the industry standard for nightclubs throughout the world. Pioneer chose Sasha to launch this ground-breaking equipment that will transform the way DJs go about their work safe in the knowledge that if he was to take the mantle in using it, then the industry would no doubt follow suit. Of course they were right as the Warehouse Project had theirs installed the week before Sasha and Digweed would take to the stage to ensure any technical gremlins could be taken care of beforehand.

The sound of Pete Tong's Essential Selection coming from my kitchen definitely signalled the start of the weekend and no matter what the weather or the state the country was in, nothing was going to dampen my spirits for the next 10 hours or so.

Arrangements had been made to meet in the centre of Manchester at one of our favourite haunts, making the taxi ride there one of excitement with talk of the last time we had seen Sasha and John play together, during their Northern Exposure tour way back in 1993 at what is now the Haçienda apartments. All nights were regaled with passion and delight by me, Gareth and Smithy as we recited favourite tracks and how music has changed for better or for worse.

After quite a few beers and banter, it was now time to head down to Store Street and the underground car park that has become part of Manchester folklore. The Warehouse Project entrance was strewn with touts selling tickets at more than double the face value, ironically only yards away from a large police contingent that was spread along the length of the street due to the large queues spilling over into the road.

A constant procession of black cabs dropped off groups of all types of clubbers young and old, all eager to get inside and out of the cold wind that whistled down the dimly lit, arched street. Thankfully our

Epilogue

wait was a matter of seconds as I met Sasha and Kirsty with her clipboard, in their usual prominent positions at front of house. A warm greeting was as ever forthcoming. They never fail to make us feel as though we are being welcomed into their own house, such is their enthusiasm and passion for something they have built up from nothing. And thank God I got to know them at an early stage.

I had already sent a text to Sasha wishing him luck for the night, not that he ever needs it, but I know how much he appreciates support and positive feedback from his peers and friends. His reply was as usual short and to the point. "Thanks mate, hope you enjoy the new stuff." I was in no doubt I would.

We are never the earliest arrivals and that had its downside tonight as we had missed the majority of James Zabiela's set. However, walking into a packed club as he reached the peak does get you instantly head-nodding and foot-tapping and before we got to the bar, we found ourselves with arms in the air as the lights beat with the crescendo of one of his last tracks. James was visibly enjoying not only the impulsive crowd but also the new set up as he bounded about behind the new CDJ2000's, mixer and his signature Gater FX controller that produces noises and sounds that only James can make.

Our appetites had been well and truly whetted and I wanted to get to see Sasha before he and John took to the floor, so we headed for the wristbanded section at the side of the stage. The VIP area has thankfully got better with each passing year and you don't have to queue for the toilet, so it's very important to gain entry to this area.

Kirsty had given us gold wristbands on entry meaning we could get close to the action without actually taking to the stage, unless you are me. As most of my friends will testify and as I've said before, I tend to get where water can't. Sasha's tour manager and long-time friend Harley Moon had with him some triple A passes which basically meant you could hand Sasha his CDs on stage if needed. Needless to say I managed to get one and headed towards the side entrance to the backstage area.

The first person I came across was Renaissance head honcho Geoff Oakes who always looks as if he's just flown in from some cool European city and probably has. I probably bump into Geoff maybe once every other year, be it at a festival, club night or awards ceremony, but it's always reassuring when he acknowledges those

God is a DJ*

who've been around from the beginning and is always happy to converse on your comings and goings with a genuine interest.

Young Zabiela stood not far away having finished his set, but he was too preoccupied in Sasha and John's set up to converse in any pleasantries.

From this vantage point you get to see the packed crowd at their most animated. Some opt for the head down approach, really in the zone and focusing on every beat, whereas others look to the sky savouring each key change.

Unified hands in the air were brought to the fore with the prolific Paula Pedroza's *Onde Esta*, a massive echoing house monster that throbs and chants into a real state of ecstasy and sent the crowd into an absolute frenzy with people pogo-ing as they did to punk records back in the Seventies. And as I've said before, when Sasha jumps, everybody jumps. The beautiful Brazilian DJ and producer, resident in Pacha Brazil, has become a staple of Sasha's more recent sets, Sasha opened his set for the 500th Essential Mix on BBC with her track *ANJOS*, one hell of a compliment for a first-time producer to receive. The feedback from the crowd's visible reaction to this track made me realise that the feeling of being a DJ is definitely up there with being the frontman of a rock band.

John Digweed, stood only feet away from Sasha, was visibly itching to play the next record to keep the crowd on a high. Both of them played three or four tracks each before letting the other one try and outdo the last, which ensured they brought out the best in each other and left the crowd wanting more.

The first track I recognised from John's set list was his own new production with studio partner Nick Muir. *Satellite* is an intense, roaring piece of electronic house music with a nasty bass loop that left Sasha nodding in approval. Such records prove to me time and again that I would always find it extremely difficult to be a DJ as there is no better place to hear great house music than in the middle of the dance floor and at that point in the night I decided to rejoin my mates to be where the magic happens.

As the night picked up pace, both DJs brought the best out of each other, John brandishing one of his Bedrock classics with a new Nic Fanculli remix of Saint's and Sinners' Pushin Too Hard that induces the crowd into raptures with its progressive chugging bassline.

Epilogue

After four hours of the finest house music brought to us by two of the finest DJs of their generation at the peak of their powers, I was intrigued as to how they could bring this incredible night to an end. The last track played out and the lights went up to a rapturous applause from the remaining 1,500 or so die-hard fans who wanted to stay and savour every minute.

Most bands go off stage at the end of their sets and return with an encore. Not many DJs can pull this off, but with Sasha and John we are always left wanting more.

Sasha left the honours to John to bring the crowd to a level they probably didn't realise they had. The press of the play button ignited the crowd again as the opening throbbing synth stabs of controversial French duo Justice's *Phantom* broke the silence and each rising chord developed into a tumultuous crescendo and assured dance floor frenzy.

Yet there was still more to come as John Lydon's unmistakable vocal cut through the PA system leaving everyone with no doubt that the last track of this epic night would be Leftfield's classic *Open Up*. Almost 20 years old, this track is without doubt one of those timeless classics from the prolific early Nineties where so much of today's house music has taken its foundations from. Thankfully, I've been an ever present throughout this period and will no doubt enjoy telling my daughter about some bloke called Sasha.

As someone profoundly said:

Life is not measured by the amount of breaths you take but by the amount of times your breath gets taken away.

This has happened to me on countless occasions thanks to the music played to me by Sasha.

As ephemeral as the lifespan of vinyl, surely the digital template for the future of house music has been borne out by a DJ who even God would take pleasure in doing a warm up set for.

Here's to the next time . . .

Track Listing

This listing is mainly from memory with some research and opinions thrown in so therefore cannot be guaranteed 100 per cent, but then what can?

Delight
Shelley's Laserdome, Longton, Stoke, 1990/91

BM-EX – *Appolonia*
PKA – *Temperatures Rising*
Brothers In Rhythm – *Such A Good Feeling*
Orbital – *Belfast*
Beloved – *Only Your Love Takes Me Higher*

Solstice
Manchester Academy, July 1991

Zoë – *Sunshine On A Rainy Day*
SLD – *Getting Out*
Corina – *Temptation*
DSK – *What Would We Do?*
Sabrina Johnston – *Peace*
K-Klass – *Rhythm is a Mystery*

Haçienda Night
Ministry of Sound, London, 1992

Havana – *Ethnic Prayer*
Sunscreem – *Love You More*
Mother – *All Funked Up*
De Niro – *Disco Evangelists*

Harmony
Haçienda, Manchester, 1992

E-lustrious – *Dance No More*
Liason D – *Future FJP*
Playtime Tunes – *Shakers Song*

Track Listing

Moby – *Go*
Joe Smooth – *Promised Land*
Fast Eddie – *Can U Dance*

Up Yer Ronson / SOAK
Corn Exchange, Leeds, 1992/93

Gloria Estefan – *Live For Loving You*
SAS – *Amber Groove*
Glam – *Hell's Party*
Dina Carroll – *Ain't No Man* (DMC mix)
Within A Dream – *Where Is The Feeling?*
Rusty – *Everything is Gonna Change* (Sasha remix)
Jimi Polo – *Better Days* (Sasha remix)
Clivilles and Cole – *Pride* (A Deeper Love)

Venus/Renaissance
Nottingham/Mansfield, June 1993

Sasha/Danny Campbell – *Together*
Hardfloor – *Acperience*
Mombassa – *Cry Freedom*
Age of Love – *Age of Love*
Felix – *Don't You Want Me?*
Djaimin – *Give You*
Brothers Loves Dubs – *The Mighty Ming*

Cream and the Big Apple
1995–2002

Sasha – *Higher Ground/Magic*
VOAT – *Moonchild*
Leftfield – *Song of Life*
Sasha – *Cloud Cuckoo*
BT – *Embracing the Sunshine* and *Remember* (Sasha mixes)

Bedrock First Birthday
Heaven, London, 1999

Bedrock – *Heaven Scent*
Saints & Sinners – *Pushin' Too Hard*

God is a DJ*

Luzon – *Bagiou Track*
Bluefish – *One*

We Love Sundays
Space, Ibiza, September 2000–2002

Datar – *B*
Underworld – *Cowgirl*
Sasha/Emerson – *Scorchio*
Groove Armada – *Superstylin*
Sunscreem – *Perfect Motion*
Orange Lemon – *Dreams of Santa Anna*

Midweek Session
Club Code, Birmingham, October 2000

Depeche Mode – *It's No Good*
Bedrock – *Voices*
Trisco – *Muzak*
Schiller – *Das Glockenspiel*
Minimalistix – *Struggle for Pleasure*
Sasha – *Xpander*

Tribal Sessions
Sankeys Soap, Manchester, 2001–2003

Cosmos – *Take Me with You*
Depeche Mode – *Freelove* (Deep Dish mix)
Funk D'Void – *Diabla*
Dot Allison – *We're Only Science* (Slam mix)
Sasha – *Xpander/Cowgirl*
Futureshock – *Frequency*
Sasha/Junkie XL – *Beauty Never Fades*

Circus
Masque, Liverpool, June 2005

Guerillaz – *Feel Good Inc/Wavy Gravy*
The Killers – *Mr Brightside* (Thin White Duke remix)
Moby – *Raining Again*/Thomas Newman – *Drive Away*

Track Listing

Epilogue
The Warehouse Project, Manchester, 2006–2009

2006
Chemical Brothers – *Out Of Control* (Sasha's Club Mix Instrumental)
Laurent Garnier – *Crispy Bacon* (King Unique Mix)
Cubic – *Superflyin'* (Bassline)
Kosmas Epsilon – *Lovesong* (Dub Mix)

2007
Swayzak – *Smile & Receive* (Apparat Remix)
Davis and May – *Neotron* (Ryan Davis Edit)
Sasha – *Park It In The Shade/Mongoose* (Original Mix)
Davis and May – *Neotron*

2008
Butch – *1,000 Lords* (Zoo Brazil Remix)
Apparat – *Arcadia* (Sasha remix)
Fairmont – *I Need Medicine*
Guy J – *Esperanza*

2009
Digweed and Muir – *Satellite*
Paula Pedroza – *Onde Esta*
Justice – *Phantom*
Leftfield – *Open Up*

DISCOGRAPHY

Original Production

B.M.EX.	*Appolonia*	UCR
Sasha & Danny Campbell	*Together*	FFRR
Sasha & Sam Mollison	*Higher Ground*	Deconstruction
Sasha & Sam Mollison	*Magic*	Deconstruction
Sasha	*The Qat Collection*	Deconstruction
Sasha	*The Qat: Remix Collection*	Deconstruction
Sasha	*The Remixes*	Arctic
Sasha with Maria Nayler	*Be As One*	Deconstruction
Sasha	*Arkham Asylum*	Deconstruction
Sasha	*Ohmna*	Deconstruction
Sasha & BT	*Heart of Imagination*	Deconstruction
Sasha	*The Other Side*	Deconstruction
Sasha & BT (as Two Phat Cunts)	*Ride*	Yoshitoshi
Sasha & BT	*Dark One*	Real World
Sasha & BT	*Warrior Song*	Real World
Sasha & BT	*Cry To The World*	Real World
Sasha	*Xpander*	Deconstruction
Sasha	*Belfunk*	Deconstruction
Sasha	*Rabbitweed*	Deconstruction
Sasha	*Baja*	Deconstruction
Sasha	*Lupus Lullaby*	Deconstruction
Sasha & Emerson	*Scorchio*	Deconstruction
Sasha	*Airdrawndagger*	Kineti
Sasha & Junkie XL	*Beauty Never Fades*	DMC

DJ Mix CDs

Sasha / CJ Mackintosh	*Mixmag Live*	DMC
Sasha	*DJ Culture Vol. 1*	Stress
Sasha and Digweed	*Renaissance*	Six6
BT	*IMA (Voyage of Ima)*	Perfecto
Various	*Radio 1 Essential Mix*	London
San Francisco	*Global Underground 9*	
Sasha and Digweed	*Northern Exposure*	Ministry of Sound
Sasha and Digweed	*Northern Exposure 2*	Ministry of Sound
Sasha and Digweed	*Expeditions*	Incredible/Sony
Ibiza	*Global Underground 13*	
Sasha and Digweed	*Communicate*	Incredible/Sony
Sasha	*Involver*	Global Underground

Discography

Sasha	*Fundacion*	Global Underground
Sasha	*Avalon Los Angeles*	LIVE 24/06/06
Sasha	*The EMFIRE Collection*	Renaissance
Sasha	*New Emissions of Light and Sound*	
Sasha	*Invol2ver*	Global Underground

Remix and Additional Production

Evolution	*Came Outta Nowhere*	Positive Vinyl
Creative Thieves	*Nasty Rhythm*	Stress
Donna Gardner	*Good Thing*	Virgin
Marina Van Rooy	*Let You Go*	Deconstruction
Urban Soul	*Alright*	Cooltempo
Urban Soul	*Always*	Cooltempo
Orbital	*Midnight*	London
Evolution	*Metropolis*	Positive Vinyl
Brothers in Rhythm	*Peace and Harmony*	Stress/Island
Unique 3	*No More*	Ten Records
Pet Shop Boys	*West End Girls*	Parlophone
Mr. Fingers	*Closer*	MCA
Ozo	*Anambra*	Riot Records
Rusty	*Everything's Gonna Change*	Stress
M People	*Someday*	Deconstruction
D-Ream	*U R The Best Thing*	FXU
Hysterix/Coloursound	*Talk To Me*	Deconstruction
E-Zee Posse	*Love on Love*	Virgin
Londonbeat	*Sea of Tranquility*	BMG
M People	*How Can I Love You More?*	Deconstruction
Judy Cheeks	*Real Deal (So in Love)*	Positiva
Alexander O'Neal	*In The Middle*	A & M
Sounds Of Blackness	*I'm Going All The Way*	A & M
Jomanda	*Never*	Warner Bros.
Eat Static	*Gulf Breeze*	Planet Dog
Hedningarna	*Krupolska*	China
Womack & Womack	*Secret Star*	WEA
Cabana Ballando	*Con Lobos*	Hi-Life
BT	*Embracing The Sunshine*	Perfecto
Up Yer Ronson	*Lost In Love*	Polydor
Seal	*I'm Alive*	ZTT
Reese Project	*Direct Me*	Nettwerk
Horse	*Careful*	Stress
BT	*Remember*	Perfecto
Gus Gus	*Purple*	4AD
Madonna	*Drowned World/Sky Fits Heaven*	Maverick
Madonna	*Ray of Light*	Maverick
Chemical Brothers	*Out of Control*	Virgin

God is a DJ*

Orbital	*Belfast*	London FFRR
U.N.K.L.E.	*In A State*	Mo Wax
Cirque De Soleil	*Pokinoi*	BMG
Faithless	*Insomnia*	BMG
Depeche Mode	*Precious*	Mute

A huge and sincere thanks to:

Chris & Becci Blood, Sasha & Zoie Coe, Richard Warburton, Gareth, Nicola, Thea & Lottie Compton-Jones, Phil Birchall, Sean Bate/Devino, Dave 'Sol' Watson, Ian 'Cass' Cassidy, Mark Smith, Pete Tilley, Craig Little, Paul Mathison, Conal & Kevin Duffy, Vernon Kay & Tess Daly, Karl Barker, Phil 'Crafty' Smart, Paul Wilkinson, Jennie Donaldson, Alex Kirkley, Nigel Clucas, Brian Cheetham, Gary Lomas, Jamie Murphy, Jason Poole, Paul Hancock, Jeni Harvey, Nicola Stephenson, Alex James, Phil Ribchester, Sy Whitehall and Beth, Mike Keat, Archie Easton, Russ&Kengo@Cuban Brothers, Tom Findlay, Andy Cato, Mad Mike, Suddi Raval & Daisy, Leroy Richardson, Rachel Lydon, Ross Mackenzie, Dee Brewster, Greg Fenton, Knuckles, Morales, Humphries, Sanchez, James Zabiela, Sparrow, Marie, John Perry, Tony Lyndop RIP, Simon Franks, Tom Dinsdale, George Lamb

My wonderful Mum, I miss you more and more and think about all the time. You still make me smile xxx

My favourite girls in the whole world – my wife Karen Blood for supporting me through thick and thin and my beautiful daughter Isla Monica Blood for lighting up my life xxx

My Dad for being there, supporting me and giving me the music!

Contributors

Dave Haslam, Elliot Eastwick, Gary McLarnan, Clare Woodcock, James Barton, Gill Nightingale, Dean Belcher, Dom Phillips, Steve Lawler, James Baillie, Tony Hannon, Buckley Boland, Sacha Lord-Marchionne, Kirsty Smith, SamKandel@WarehouseProject, Rich Mcginnis, Pete Tong, Yousef, Kim@idm, John Digweed, Tim Sheridan, Smokin Jo, Mike Pickering, Graeme Park, Paul Kane, Paul Myers, Steve Parry, Brian Cheetham, Jamie Scahill, Mark Hogg, Geoff Oakes, Brett Lowther, Pete Gooding, Danny Whitehead, Jason Bull, Tara Morgan, Dee, Claire & everyone@Excession, Paul Irwin & everyone at Cube Media, Harley Moon, Lisa Horan, Sheryl Garratt, Jane Bussmann, Bill Broughton, Frank Brewster, Boys Own, Fiona Cartledge, Charlie Chester, Darren Hughes, Dave Beer, Ben Turner, Lindsay Barchan@lindsaybrachan.co.uk, Rachel Esson@Night Magazine, Ron Slomovicz@dancemusic.about.com, Paula Pedroza, Norman Hines, Martin Wells, IBIZA, NEW YORK AND MIAMI!

Photos Courtesy Of:

Dean Belcher – *see* www.deanbelcherphotographer.com
Jason Warth – *see* www.jasonwarth.com
Sal Badalucco
Clodagh Maguire
Angela Collins
Paula Pedroza

Recommended Reading

Dave Haslam – *Manchester, England*
Dave Haslam – *Adventures on the Wheels of Steel*
Sheryl Garratt – *Adventures in Wonderland*
Jane Bussmann – *Once in a Lifetime*
Frank Broughton/Bill Brewster – *Last Night a DJ Saved My Life*
Peter Hook – *How Not to Run a Club*
Tim Lawrence – *Love Saves the Day*
Sean Bidder – *Pump up the Volume*
Vince Alletti – *The Disco Files 73–78*

Contributors

Recommended Sites

www.djsasha.com
www.johndigweed.com
www.warehouseproject.com
www.djstevelawler.com
www.bedrock.org.uk
www.globalunderground.co.uk
www.excession.co.uk
www.aceofclubspresents.co.uk
www.residentadvisor.net
www.ibiza-voice.com
www.deanbelcherphotographer.com
www.tribalgathering.co.uk
www.circusclub.com
www.essentialselection.co.uk
www.petetong.com
www.creamfields.com
www.lindsaybarchan.co.uk
www.fabriclondon.com
www.jameszabiela.com
www.dancemusic.about.com
www.jasonwarth.com
www.thecubanbrothers.com
www.hotelesvive.com
www.paulapedroza.com
www.ourmaninthefield.com